'T **BAD ASS** BIBLE

THE BAD ASS BIBLE

AN ESSENTIAL GUIDE FOR MEN

Red Brick Press
New York

S. K. Smith

Red Brick Press
Hatherleigh Press
5–22 46ᵗʰ Avenue
Long Island City, NY 11101
1-800-528-2550

Library of Congress Cataloging-in-Publication data available upon request.

All Hatherleigh Press titles are available for special promotions and premiums. For more information, please contact the manager of our Special Sales department at 800-528-2550.

Cover & interior designed by Scott Anderson & Tai Blanche
Illustrations by Sebastian Conley
Printed in Canada on acid-free paper
10 9 8 7 6 5 4 3 2 1

Disclaimer:
This is a joke book, you moron. Don't try this stuff at home.

To **LEE MARVIN**,
*patron saint
of badasses*

BADASS
TABLE OF CONTENTS

HOW TO READ THIS BOOK

The badass is an American original, like Lucky Strikes or muscle cars. From Lee Marvin to Vin Diesel, the badass is the epitome of the American male.

Badasses radiate confidence in everything they do, whether it's dealing with women, ordering a drink, or buying a set of wheels. The badass knows how to walk the Walk and talk the Talk. He's slow to anger, but brutally efficient when fighting back.

The badass is all about fundamentals. That's what makes him stand out like a sore thumb in today's culture of excess—the badass sticks to essentials.

The goal of *The Badass Bible* is to fill you in on those essentials. The badass way to walk. The badass way to talk. What to wear. What to eat. What to drive. Where to go for entertainment. It's a sourcebook you can refer to again and again, as circumstances demand.

Chapter by chapter, page by page, we dissect and explain badass style. By book's end, you should have absorbed everything you need to know to project badass attitude in everything you do—from changing your tires to walking your dog.

The true meaning of "badass" is a riddle, wrapped in an enigma—*The Badass Bible* is here to help you solve it.

Compiling *The Badass Bible* is a complex, some might say even foolhardy, undertaking, like scaling Everest wearing Converse canvas high tops or wrestling an alligator with a trout stuffed down your pants. Misguided. Delusional.

But absolutely necessary. Now, more than ever.

What follows is a Badass Baedeker, a field guide to the wild, the untamed, the defiant Badass. Like the Yeti, the badass is hairy, mysterious, seldom spotted. But one sighting will change your life. The badass offers us a glimpse of

an earlier, wilder time. It's an encounter with our undiluted, brutal origins.

Read it slowly, in good light, without moving your lips. Focus not only on the information imparted, but on its gist, on the essence of the language.

This is not bathroom reading. This is not a book you want falling out of your back pocket, gym bag or briefcase. Cherish it, hoard it, protect it.

This book may save your miserable life.

AN ETHOS FOR OUR TROUBLED TIMES

Badass.

Something clicks deep in human brain-stem tissue when the word is uttered. Badass. Like wolf howls and fire, it stirs dark, primal memories.

Back when early man squatted in caves, naked and malnourished, terrified of his own shadow, there were a select few, an elite handful of men who ventured beyond the cave's mouth to take on the Big Unknown. Were they stronger, faster, or taller? Not necessarily. What these few possessed can be a called prehistoric attitude, Stone Age chutzpah, or good old-fashioned guts. With nary a grunt, they fanned out across our lawless planet, kicking Paleolithic butt, taking names and making the world safe for the huddled masses. They were the originals. They were "Badass."

Historians assure us that a blood-red line—jagged, raw, like a knife scar—wends its way across our collective Past. Viking. Inca. Norman. Mongol. Apache. Mountain Man. Pioneer. Cowboy. Veteran. Generation after generation of men who knew how to fight, to love, to grill meat, and to kill with their bare hands if necessary. Call it our Badass Heritage.

They're still among us, badasses, men of every size, color, nationality, and religion. You see them in bars, at the track, picking up their kids from school. That deadly calm, that unerring self-assurance. Badasses. Men, as Staff Sergeant Barry Sadler used to sing, "who mean just what they say."

A timeless style. An eternal aura. An attitude of confidence and cool that knows no era.

Today's badass is the last of the rugged individuals. Heir to the samurai and the gunfighter. Descendant of the mountain men and the knights errant.

In our era of mass homogenization and commodification, that makes him Public Enemy Number One.

Open your eyes and look around you. Instead of diversity, the early twenty-first century offers us redundant abundance, more and more and even more of the same damn thing. We are smothered in brightly-packaged sameness—how many Starbucks or Gaps are necessary to keep us from feeling deprived? Captains of Industry are thoroughly prepared to keep throwing new franchises at us, strip mall after strip mall, until we stand up and cry, "All right, already!"

A badass will lead the way.

The badass has a natural aversion to the shills and three-card monte players we call advertising men, CEOs, and politicians. What they call "branding," the badass calls brain-washing.

Like some lonely mountaineer trekking across the face of Everest, the badass carves his own path. He wears, drives, drinks, watches, and listens to what he chooses, when he chooses, where he chooses, uninfluenced by fads or advertising campaigns. "Badass style" is understated but instantly recognizable. Like a chopped Harley or a good pair of sunglasses: simple, direct, and functional.

The sad truth is, badasses are an endangered species. Their habitats, the decrepit boxing rings and half-lit dive bars where they thrive, are slowly disappearing. Whenever an all-night burrito stand is razed and a "Big Box" chain store constructed, a little bit of the world's store of "badass" is lost forever.

It's time to reverse that trend.

THE TEN BADASS COMMANDMENTS

1. Thou shalt assume the worst of every man, and the best of every woman.

The sexual politics of the badass are refreshingly primitive. Men are lustful, violent louts who are not to be trusted. Women look, smell, and act better in all ways, all the time. There is no doubt that woman is still the better, more powerful half of the species. That's what Friedrich Nietzsche meant when he opined, "When you go to woman, bring the whip." What never gets quoted is the rest of his aphorism: "Then hand it to her and accept your punishment."

Truth be told, the Achilles heel of any badass, that most vulnerable of all spots, is the heart. The badass, child of nature, friend of man, can always be brought low by love. Like King Kong (a lovesick badass if ever there was one), the badass Beast is always conquered by Beauty.

2. Thou shalt not smile when a sneer will do.

As Desmond Morris demonstrated in *The Naked Ape,* his seminal study of human behavior, a smile is a primate sexual signal, intended to reveal the health of one's teeth to a potential mate. Dumb move in a bar fight. Better to grimace like a Maori warrior. Or channel Richard Widmark in *Kiss Of Death*—check out his maniacal sneer as he pushes the invalid old woman down the flight of stairs.

3. Thou shalt not run when you can walk.

A badass never hurries. Remember the ineffable calm of Roger Duchesne in Jean-Pierre Melville's classic of cool, *Bob le Flambeur?* The French have a phrase for it: *sang froid.* Cold blood. Cool as a cucumber. Hemingway called it "grace under pressure." The badass masters the situation. Never the reverse. Wife's impending childbirth? A vicious attack of Montezuma's Revenge? A transatlantic flight pulling away from the gate? It will wait.

4. Thou shalt wear shorts only when working out.

Shorts are for little kids, basketball players, and mailmen. Even Kobe wears long pants when he's out and about.

5. Thou shalt never use the stubble head on an electric razor.

The "two-day's growth" look must be come by naturally, even if that involves making oneself scarce during clean-shaven days. And gentlemen, never, under any circumstances, use a woman's disposable plastic razor to shave your face. They nick.

6. Thou shalt never be seen on a bicycle, skateboard or in-line skates. Neither shalt thou be seen driving a Volkswagen Bug or Mini Cooper.

Badass vehicles burn fossil fuels. Remember that, even if you have to carve it into your forehead. The only two-wheeled contraption a badass will straddle is a four-stroke Honda 450 or a vintage 1953 Indian "Chief" motorcycle. Reissued pastel-colored "toy cars" are glorified paperweights on wheels—a badass never travels in a vehicle he or she can pick up with one hand.

7. Thou shalt shun the use of Equal, NutraSweet, and grape jelly. Neither shalt thou consume soy-based products.

A catch-all commandment governing nutrition. The Badass Diet is about nitrites, nitrites, nitrites. These days, when he looks up from his beef jerky, the badass sees himself surrounded by a sea of wobbling, flabby humanity. That ain't nitrites, Bub. It's sugars, transfats, and "natural flavors." As for soy-based products... if we wanted to eat the inner soles of our shoes, we would.

8. Thou shalt never remove or alter a tattoo.

You made your mistake. Now live with it.

9. Thou shalt never wear stripes, checks, or polkadots.

Frippery is not badass. The true badass is unassuming in his appearance, avoiding distracting logos, bangles, gewgaws, and zippers that serve no function. When dressing, the badass thinks lean and mean, with timeless lines and durable fabrics. Think Bruce Lee's karate pajamas in *Enter the Dragon* or Clint Eastwood's poncho and hat in *Fistful of Dollars*. Stealth clothing. Apparel you could fight, die, and be buried in.

10. Thou shalt never use anesthesia, painkillers or crutches.

Psychiatrists tell us pain is all in our heads (yet they're the first to double-over when slammed in the gut with a fist. Figures.) To the badass, pain is an incentive. Blood is the red flag that kicks the badass into action.

In *Hagakure: The Book of the Samurai*, a book of aphorisms for warriors written in the 1700s, there is an observation that still holds true: "If one's sword is broken, he will strike with his hands. If his hands are cut off, he will press the enemy down with his shoulders. If his shoulders are cut away, he will bite through ten or 15 enemy necks with his teeth. Courage is such a thing." Or, as Nietzsche quipped, "What does not destroy me, makes me stronger."

Now that you know the Ten Badass Commandments, it's time to learn the basics.

THE BADASS WAY TO WALK

Every subculture has its ambulatory style—think Tony Manero's swagger in *Saturday Night Fever* (somewhere between fey and exuberant); the baggy pants shuffle of hip hop *aficionados*; the praying mantis runway strut of the supermodel. For badasses, it's the "Gunfighter."

Dating back to the days of Wyatt Earp and Jesse James, the Gunfighter is a walk that communicates lethal readiness. With head and shoulders thrown back, one's arms and hands swing free. (**NOTE:** A guy with his hands in his pockets is either searching for change or deep into a round of pocket pool.) Hips are wide, with soles of the feet firmly placed on the ground. Fists should be lightly clenched.

The "Gunfighter" serves to maximize the badass's potential responses to danger. The head operates like the gun turret on a Bradley fighting vehicle, swiveling restlessly, scoping out threats. The semi-clenched fists can be quickly raised into a classic boxer's stance; the planted feet can deliver a deathblow to an opponent's esophagus in a nanosecond. Think of each step accompanied by the clink of spurs and the creak of leather, and you have a walk that essentially grabs every passerby by the lapel and shouts, "I mean business."

THE BADASS WAY TO TALK

You walk the walk, you gotta talk the talk. For badasses, it's the "Growl."

From Lee Marvin to gridiron scourge Bill Romanowski, badasses have perfected this glorified mumble, a bass rumble that hums with pit bull menace.

The Growl has two functions. First, if it's uncommunicative enough, it forces one's opponent to lean in closer to hear what's being said—close enough to be wrapped in a life-threatening headlock. Second, the bass tones say to all and sundry: I'm packing some serious love coil. That's right—like they teach you on the playground, deep voice, big package. Simple verities, people, as old as the species.

The deepest growl on record isn't going to help you, however, if you have nothing to say. The badass shuns excessive lip-flapping. Talk is cheap and silence is golden. As *The Book of the Samurai* admonishes us: "The essentials of speaking are in not speaking at all. If you think that you can finish something without speaking, finish it without saying a single word."

'Nuff said.

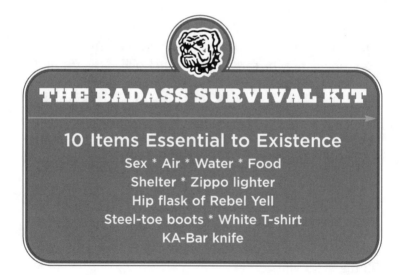

THE BADASS SURVIVAL KIT

10 Items Essential to Existence
Sex * Air * Water * Food
Shelter * Zippo lighter
Hip flask of Rebel Yell
Steel-toe boots * White T-shirt
KA-Bar knife

CHAPTER TWO

BADASS HISTORY

Nowadays, when we watch Vin Diesel swagger through yet another underwritten piece of fluff targeted at the Stridex-and-Skechers set (ages 11 to 17), we may lose sight of the fact that that swagger has an ancient pedigree. Diesel and his fellow heavies are merely the latest in a long and distinguished line of badasses, a brawny, no-nonsense legacy that stretches from early Man to the present. Any examination of the Badass must pay tribute to this august lineage; if a badass scowls and brawls anywhere in the world, it is because he walks...

IN THE FOOTSTEPS OF GIANTS

Come with us now as we stride through the ages, tracing the path blazed by badasses ancient and modern. We start with Neanderthal man—Grandaddy of 'em all.

NEANDERTHAL MAN

Anthropologists tell us that between 100,000 and 40,000 years ago, Neanderthal man hunted with stone tools, lived in caves, and used fire. Unlike his male model competitor, Cro-Magnon Man, Neanderthal was a homely fellow— large, thick skull; heavy brow ridges; sloping forehead; buck teeth; receding chin. At about five feet tall, broad-chested, injury-prone, he was probably the last guy picked for caveman dodgeball. So Neanderthal was forced to develop alternate strategies to success. He had to learn to maximize his wiry strength and nurture his natural rock-ribbed orneriness. He had to become a badass.

GENGHIS KHAN

What do you call a man who single-handedly carved out one of the greatest empires in world history, a swath of wild and wooly territory stretching from China to the Black Sea?

Boss.

Genghis Khan (1167?-1227) was a badass from Day One: Legend has it that he was born clutching a clot of his own blood. On capturing enemy fortifications, he made it a habit of executing anyone standing taller than an ox-cart axle. Historians tell us that most of the inhabitants of a region called Munchkinland survived the cut, as it were.

VLAD III, THE IMPALER

a.k.a. *Vlad Tepes* or *Dracula* ("son of Dracul," "son of The Dragon"). This fifteenth-century Romanian prince helped in the construction and fortification of Bucharest in a desperate campaign to ward off the Ottoman Turks. Despite his smoldering matinee idol looks, Vlad is said to have murdered 100,000 people by impaling them on spikes. It's widely acknowledged that his gruesome legend inspired British journalist Bram Stoker to pen his horror classic, *Dracula,* initiating a cult of celebrity few other mass murderers have enjoyed.

Countless Hammer horror movies later, few of us can look at a heaving female décolletage and bared neck and not whisper a "Thank you" to that Master of Disaster. As of this printing, there is word that the Romanian

Government is contemplating establishing a Dracula theme park in Sighisoara, Vlad's birthplace. A featured item on the park's snack bar menu will no doubt be the ever-popular Donner kebab.

WILLIAM TECUMSEH SHERMAN

The first of the modern badasses, Sherman acknowledged the awesome responsibilities that come with power. "War is hell," he opined, and the man who burned Atlanta and cut a swath of destruction across Georgia knew whereof he spoke.

Sherman embodies the badass's overriding sense of honor and self-effacement. His response to post-war entreaties to run for political office neatly summarizes badass humility and restraint. "If nominated," he replied, "I will not accept. If elected I will not serve." Badasses stick to their principles.

FRANCIS ALBERT SINATRA

Sinatra is proof positive that anyone can be a badass. Once a skinny teen heartthrob from Hoboken, New Jersey, Sinatra transformed himself into an urban legend, a force of nature, a hell of an actor and the "Chairman of the Board."

For a time in the late '50s and early '60s, Sinatra and his Rat Pack buddies ruled Glitter Gulch, defining male cool for generations to come. These days, you can't order a martini, put on a skinny tie, or ogle a sequin-gowned floozy without owing licensing fees to Sinatra & Co.

But Sinatra was more than a proto-hipster. He was a badass. Old Blue Eyes perfected the badass art of intimidation and manipulation while lifting nary a finger. Which reminds us of the Shecky Greene routine about Sinatra once saving his life. It seems a bunch of goons were working Shecky over one night in Vegas when Frank walked by. The pummeling continued until Frank muttered, "Okay, fellas, I think that's enough."

Call it badass *noblesse oblige.*

ROGER CRAIG KNIEVEL

a.k.a. *Evel Knievel.* With his own listing in the Guinness Book of World Records (for breaking 35 bones), Evel is living proof that when you mix high-octane fuel and badasses, step back. Way back.

From his barnstorming days with Evel Knievel's Motorcycle Daredevils, when he rode through walls of fire and jumped over live rattlesnakes and mountain lions, Knievel graduated to jumping parked cars and semi trucks. Could landmarks be far behind?

On New Year's Day, 1968, Knievel jumped 151 feet over the fountains at Caesar's Palace. A messy landing put him in a coma for a month—plenty of time to plan his outrageous Snake River Canyon stunt, when the parachute of his rocket-powered Skycycle caught a prevailing wind and hauled cycle and "America's Legendary Daredevil" down onto the banks of the river far below. After busting himself up jumping over a tank of live sharks in 1976, Knievel retired, adhering to that first rule of Badass Ethics: *No one can buy you a round of drinks if you're dead.*

CHARLES "HANK" BUKOWSKI

Someone once quipped that the poet W. H. Auden looked like a cake left out in the rain. If that's so, then Charles Bukowski looked like a cake left out in a hailstorm. This American original was German-born, an autodidact schooled in the arts of booze, broads, and gutterwise prose. Bukowski explored his sun-blasted demi-monde in a seemingly inexhaustible stream of novels, short stories, poems and diatribes, laying his soul bare for all to scan.

True to the badass credo, Bukowski bore his fame as gracefully as his adversity. Even defeat and writer's block smelled like opportunity to him. When asked by some acolyte how he sought out inspiration, he replied: "You don't... You don't try. That's very important: Not to try, either for Cadillacs, creation, or immortality. You wait, and if nothing happens, you wait some more. It's like a bug high on the wall. You wait for it to come to you. When it gets close enough you reach out, slap out and kill it. Or if you like its looks, you make a pet out of it."

"CLASSY" FREDDIE BLASSIE

The King (if not the Emperor) of the Heels, Blassie single-handedly embodied the crazy arc of pro wrestling in the second half of the twentieth century, from small city "smokers" cast with local talent to the media-glitz of today's WWE, with its steroid-enhanced behemoths and multi-million dollar purses. Blassie (who once wrestled a diseased bear to a draw) won his renown as The Vampire, biting and gnawing on opponents with his carefully-filed incisors. Blassie reigns high in the Badass Pantheon not only for his ruthlessness and physical prowess, but also because he actually seemed to enjoy hurting others and being hurt in return.

MR T.

From the Chicago projects to pro-wrestling to co-starring with George Peppard and Robert Vaughn on *The A Team*—no screenwriter could come up with a more unlikely career trajectory than Mr T's. T's trademark gold chains and Mohawk say more "buffoon" than "badass," but his stints as a bodyguard and pro wrestler (including a knockout of Roddy Piper) as well as his public battle with cancer, certify him as the real deal. Don't pity the fool—T's *badass*.

SAM PECKINPAH

WWII vet and one-time assistant to director Don Siegel, Peckinpah is the undisputed Master of Macho Moviemaking. With his customary biker bandanna and eye-patch, Peckinpah single-handedly set the standard for depictions of on-screen violence (*The Wild Bunch*, *Straw Dogs*) and unforgettable action set-pieces (*The Getaway*, the abandoned aircraft carrier shootout in *Killer Elite*).

A dyed-in-the-wool badass... and a hardass to boot.

"NEUTRON" JACK WELCH

You know we've entered the Renaissance of the Robber Barons when a no-holds-barred CEO like Welch can be considered a badass. (Who was the last CEO whose name even rang a bell? Lee Iacocca? Ray Kroc?) Welch's

Machiavellian corporate housecleaning helped set the merciless tone of the '90s boom. A wish-fulfillment badass for the Wall Street crowd.

BADASS—OR DUMBASS?

MIKE TYSON

Once the most-feared fighter in the heavyweight division, Tyson has had most of the good sense he was born with knocked out of him. He's become a living, breathing replica of the Comedy/Tragedy masks, alternating moment to moment between tearful self-pity and blind rage. His best bouts now take place streetside. Tonya Harding has more legitimacy as a pugilist. Dumbass.

SYLVESTER STALLONE

Rambo and *Rocky*—what are these series but cornerstones of badass popular culture? So though Stallone seems to shrink in stature with each passing year (sort of like your grandmother, eh?), his film legacy (with the exception, of course, of *Cobra*) guarantees him badass status.

BILL ROMANOWSKI

Whether it's spitting in the face of opposing players or punching out teammates, Romanowski is a poster child for testosterone overload. The trouble is, those hormones may not be his own. Bill's known for raiding his wife's medicine cabinet—who knew diet pills could make you so damn angry? A chemically-altered badass, but a badass all the same.

MARION "SUGE" KNIGHT

Suge's never in the news for civic acts, like cutting the ribbon on a new bridge or funding a wing in a children's hospital. His bailiwick seems to be brawls, parole violations, and intimidation. The closest the rap world comes to a Mafia don, he puts the "gangster" back in "gangsta."

THE BADASS WAY

TO SURVIVE A 20-FOOT DROP

In all situations, even life-threatening ones, the badass stays calm and maintains control. Panic will get you dead fast.

You're trapped in a room a couple of stories up in a burning building. The fire escapes and stairs are inaccessible, the building is about to collapse, and flames are racing across the floor toward you.

What do you do? The badass thinks in threes:
- Shorten jump
- Soften landing
- Protect skull

1. You can shorten the jump by tying bedsheets together and lowering yourself down their full length—you can subtract 6 to 10 feet from your drop this way. Hanging by one's arms from the window also helps.

2. Scan the ground below for trees, shrubs, car roofs, dumpsters—anything more flexible and for-giving than concrete or asphalt. If that fails, search for sloping ground—the force of your fall will be distributed horizontally as you roll downhill.

3. Protect your head—wrap it in towels before you jump if necessary.

4. Lower yourself as close to the ground as possible, bend your knees slightly and let go.

5. On impact, allow your knees to bend stiffly. Tumble forward, rolling and absorbing the force of the fall throughout the length of your body and protecting your head at all times.

6. Assess the damage. Unwrap your head and check for leaks. Thank whatever God you worship and get help immediately.

THE BADASS WAY

TO SURVIVE A MOTORCYCLE CRASH

Have you ever noticed how Fate has a way of asserting itself at the least convenient moments? One minute you're on your Ninja, knee down, tucked into a faultless turn, the next you're face-to-face with a drunk in a Chevy pick-up who's swerved into your lane and is bearing down on you.

You've barely got time to pop in the DVD of your life, let alone watch it flash before your eyes. If you want to add another chapter to that DVD...

1. Get rid of the bike. Lay it down, throw it down—just get it away from you.

2. Fall limp. Think "rag-doll thrown from a train." Keep your head, arms, and legs tucked in.

3. Try to roll. Let the force of your fall dissipate gradually. After impact, lay still. Wait for emergency personnel to arrive. Don't allow anyone to remove your helmet or lift your head.

3

CHAPTER THREE

BADASS STYLE

The world of fashion resembles nothing so much as those wheels caged hamsters seem compelled to run on. What looks like forward progress is in fact running in place: Repetition just seems like revolution.

Enter the badass. In a perfect world, the badass could walk around in a Ben Davis shopcoat and be done with it, but the *fashionistas* have co-opted that no-frills tog (as well as *Superfly*-era leisure suits and ersatz trucker caps), annointing it as the *look du jour*.

It's at this nexus that the badass, street-Zen master that he is, just turns his back on the whole thing. The badass would rather go naked than wear polyester hip-huggers or vintage Adidas trainers. (He'd look a hell of a lot better too.) As in all things, the badass dresses un-selfconsciously. He plans nothing; he *is*.

BADASS THREADS

BADASS PANTS

The badass expects form and function to mesh seamlessly. His pant of choice? For everyday wear, it would have to be Dickies.

C. N. Williamson and E. E. "Colonel" Dickie hit on a winning concept in 1922 and haven't veered from it. Manly and timeless. No pleats, no Easy-Fit wide-in-the-beam styling, no superfluous pockets, no vestigial tool loops. Less is always more. Drip-dry, wrinkle-proof 8¾-ounce twill. Pants to wear while camping, changing your motorcycle chain, or kicking down a bail-jumper's motel room door.

Also valued for their no-frills appeal are Levi's shrink-to-fits, the true heir to Levi Strauss and Jacob Davis' patented copper-riveted "waist overalls." Standard-issue leg-wear for grease monkeys worldwide.

However, there are times when the badass requires something even more rugged, when the welter of circumstance demands that you kneel on broken glass, say, or take a round of birdshot in the thigh. That's when Bailey's "Wild-Ass" logger work pants or Carhartt double-knee duck work dungarees come in handy. Both are the closest you can come these days to wearing chainmail.

Then there's the question of leather pants. As we'll see, leathers emerged from the world of motorcycle riding sometime in the 1960s. (One theory holds that the crossbreeding of California Hells Angels and musicians gave birth to the style; another is that it dates back to the Mods and Rockers strife in England.) Whatever the case, once Jim Morrison sported them onstage (if only briefly; Jim liked to expose himself), leather pants were eagerly adopted by the music world, becoming a *de rigeur* article of rock star clothing.

The sad truth is, wearing leathers is no longer just for bikers or rockers. Like all good things, leather pants have been co-opted by the cultural lemmings. Teenage girls with braces and veteran couch potatoes can buy a pair at the local leather outlet. Is nothing sacred?

BADASS UNDERWEAR

Badasses wear underwear for one reason and one reason only: to prevent chafing and fungus infections. In a perfect world, there'd be nothing between the badass and his Dickies, so to speak. But this world ain't perfect.

Good underwear breathes. And fresh air is the mortal enemy of jock itch. Think cotton. The badass avoids silks, thermal synthetics, wool. They're nothing but high-priced fungus incubators. He favors boxers for their roominess, and because they can double as a bathing suit in a pinch.

NOTE: *Never, under any circumstances, does the badass wear bikini briefs. There is conclusive scientific evidence that bikini briefs raise your base scrotal temperature and kill spermatozoa. So, unless you like your little guys soft-boiled, skip the "Marc Spitzes." Besides, they'd make even Bronko Nagurski look like a pool boy in the South of France. A badass fashion "Don't."*

BADASS SHIRTS

Like all badass apparel, shirts must meet the twin criteria of functionality and comfort.

A badass shirt must leave the hands and arms free to move. It must be quick "wicking," capable of aiding in stanching the flow of blood from an open wound, whether your own or another's. And it must be durable, with enough tensile strength to be used as a tourniquet, restraint, or impromptu means of escape. It must be free of buttons, zippers, pockets, and any other encumbrances.

We're talking T-shirts—BVD, Fruit of the Loom, Hanes. Cool, durable, efficient. Once considered mere underwear, the T-shirt has come out of the closet, as it were, emerging as the top of choice for the badass. It doesn't matter if your suggested colors are at the fuschia or mauve end of the spectrum, badasses stick with the monochromatic "dog-vision gray scale:" black, gray, white. Blue for variety.

NOTE: *Logos are to be avoided—why let the bastards advertise their product on your chest? Let 'em rent a sandwich board. Hipsters and rock musicians seem to have cornered the low-end market on shirts hawking mid-American eateries, towing services and long-shut bowling alleys. Cheap import knock-offs with misspelled slogans ("2 Fast 2 Ferous") are to be shunned. And never, ever, sport a T-shirt that has been handpainted or had its message ironed on in the local mall. You might as well paint a target on your chest.*

Badasses have two other options when it comes to upper-body wear—the wife-beater T-shirt and the cut-off button-down.

The wife-beater or "muscle tee" has had very specific socio-economic associations for decades now (See *Badass Ethnic Types*). Once seen as an essential component of Italian-American inner city summer wear, the wife-beater emerged from the Brooklyn–Queens micro-climate sometime in the '50s, in the person of Marlon Brando's Stanley Kowalski. Brando popularized the wife-beater, doing for the string tee what Brigitte Bardot did for the bikini—making it standard-issue garb for raging hormonal cases worldwide. When the *fashionistas* discarded the wife-beater and chased off after hippie paisleys and corduroys, badasses reclaimed their rightful possession. Today, sported by the likes of Kid Rock and Vin Diesel, the wife-beater is back where it belongs—gracing the biceps of the truly badass.

The cut-off button-down has a more complicated pedigree. Some have argued that it dates back to the Pacific campaign during World War II—delirious from the humidity and heat, sailors would tear off the sleeves of their blue denim fatigues to cool down. Others point out that the cut-off was popular with construction workers in the mid-'60s (an association exploited and, yes, made tragicomic by gay cultural phenomenon, The Village People). Whatever the case, beware: The cut-off shirt borders on the over-demonstrative. It tries too hard, showing just the kind of fashion effort and consciousness badasses shun. If your sleeves are torn off fighting a hunger-crazed grizzly, that's one thing, but to sit down and purposefully tear the arms off a perfectly good shirt—that's something teenage girls do.

BADASS OUTERWEAR

Like all things "badass," badass outerwear should be minimalist and functional, offering efficient protection in a lean and mean world.

Wool, leather and denim are the only acceptable materials. Unnecessary belts, flaps, pockets, and zippers could be the very items that put you in harm's way (in the wrong hands, that sash can be transformed into a garotte). Furs and other synthetic materials (particularly anything shiny) will make you the object of ridicule, if not worse.

When one thinks of classic badass outerwear, less is always more. There's Steve McQueen escaping the POW camp wearing just a sweatshirt. Robert Mitchum cinching his trench coat tighter in *Out of the Past*. Or Marlon Brando's leather jacket in *The Wild One*.

A contemporary version of these badass classics is, without a doubt, the Carhartt chore coat. Made out of tough-as-nails cotton duck, blanket-lined, the Carhartt coat is the quintessence of "rugged outerwear," the choice of movie grips, stevedores, and snowmobilers worldwide. If one badass motto is "Never let 'em see you sweat," another has to be "Never let 'em see you shiver."

A Short History of the Leather Jacket

Stop John Q. Public on the street and ask him the distinguishing feature of badass garb and you know what he'll say? "Leather jacket."

For once, John Q. Public is right. Our research indicates that the badass–animal skin outerwear nexus goes way back. Neanderthal man in untanned hides. Inca warriors in jerkins made out of jaguar pelts. Our badass forebears draped themselves in the skins of vanquished prey, hoping to acquire some measure of their cunning and grace.

The leather jacket *per se* first crops up as badass accouterment with Davy Crockett. His fringed suede jacket and hatchet ensemble caused quite a stir in soirees from Washington, DC, to the Alamo. A sharp-shootin', bar-rasslin' tradition that would make any badass proud.

After disappearing from vogue, the leather jacket resurfaced out of thin air, literally. World War I fighting aces favored the leather jacket for its pliancy, warmth, and water-repellant qualities. On the muddy ground down below, motorcycle messengers wore leather jackets to protect them from roadside hazards.

Time and specialization drove the two designs further and further apart. By the end of World War II, the A-2 flight jacket was being manufactured out of a brown-toned goatskin (due to rationing), while the motorcycle jacket featured a short, belted waist, diagonal zippers, and special pads for kidney protection.

It's at this point that the flight jacket disappears from our story. The motorcycle jacket, on the other hand, explodes into notoriety. With the post-war boom in motorcycle manufacturing and use, as well as the spate of biker-themed B-movies (courtesy of Roger Corman and Marlon Brando), the leather jacket became identified with youth, rebellion, speed, and grease. Its subsequent adoption by rockers, punks, and other misfits has served only to cement that association.

NOTE: *While "leathers" has become a catch-all term for motorcycle outerwear, a badass would never be caught wearing actual racing leathers—the brightly-colored, skin-tight garb can make even the baddest badass look like a stunt extra in a Power Rangers episode.*

The typical badass leather jacket is made of black leather softened with age. It does double-duty as pillow, brawl-aid (toss it over opponent's head, then wallop), water container, wound dressing, and impromptu wedding gift. The leather jacket is to the badass what his hat is to the cowboy—indispensible, essential, irreplaceable. A best friend who can't talk.

BADASS TREADS

What's wrong with the following Badass true-life scenario?

Badass John Doe is in a hell-hole of a neighborhood (pit bulls, broken glass, cars on blocks on front lawns). He's three minutes into repossessing a late-on-payment 2004 Honda Civic and that's two minutes too many. It ain't going well. The master key isn't working.

Suddenly, the owner's porch light flashes on. A bullmastiff lunges down the front steps and a Hulk-sized silhouette fills the doorway behind it. It's flee or fight time and Badass chooses fight. He stands, fists clenched, his feet tense in their Tevas...

Easy, right? Badasses don't wear sandals. Leave the sandals to itinerant Buddhist monks and slacker kayaker types. A naked foot is a vulnerable foot. Nothing open-toed, either—unless you want to be mistaken for a Dutch tourist. Similarly, anything that slips on can slip off. That can take the sting out of even the most deadly flying kick.

Athletic shoes may give you a slight footspeed edge, but they put you at a distinct disadvantage in most street fights—one good stomp by your opponent and you'll be doubled-over in pain, your insteps seriously bruised if not shattered. Leave the Shaq spaceship silver high-tops where they belong, on the playground.

Stick with boots. A good boot provides support for the ankles and arches. A great boot can serve as a lethal weapon. Which is why the badass likes his boots with steel toes. A well-placed shot at your opponent's temple, kidneys, or throat and you've instantly gained the upper hand (or foot, as it were).

Red Wings are classic industrial-strength work boots with a raft of extras—protection against electrical hazards, a stainless steel midsole to withstand punctures. All of which adds weight and conviction to a good stomp. Equally convincing in a free-for-all are Red Dawg forester boots, made by lumberjack outfitter Bailey's—the spikes in their Vibram soles (designed to prevent slipping in forest mud) will provide all the extra emphasis you need.

What about Doc Martens? you ask. There are, it seems, rabid devotees of the English boot. Most of them, however, sport neon-tinted Mohawks and pierced eyebrows. The "1460," with its distinctive yellow web stitching and black-and-yellow heel loop, is footwear for kids—angry, pierced, headbanging kids, but kids nonetheless.

Okay. You're clothed and protected from the elements. Now for the good stuff.

BADASS SHADES

They say the eyes are the windows of the soul. Badass, draw those blinds! If your opponent can see your eyes, you may have given him all the motivational edge he needs. Ask a motorcycle cop why he wears mirrored shades all the time and you know what he'll tell you? Because it scares the crap out of the perps. All that suspect can see when he looks in your eyes is his own terrified reflection.

Make 'em sweat. A good pair of shades can make you seem... inhuman, a real-life Terminator.

The right sunglasses are an essential part of the badass wardrobe. They can aid and abet his air of invincibility. They should be light-weight, flexible and UV-filtering.

Brands? Go for the best: Ray-Ban and Bolle. Started in 1937 to equip aviators, Ray-Ban has been the industry standard ever since. Bolle's shades are state-of-the-art, favored by ball players and extreme sportsmen worldwide.

Style? As with all things badass, make them lean and mean. Leave the "Jackie-O" look to your Aunt Sylvie in Jupiter Beach—shades should make you look resolute, focussed, inevitable.

BADASS FASHION TIP

Never remove your shades in public. It's like Samson having his locks shorn. Once an adversary has seen your unprotected eyes, the intimidative power of the eyewear is destroyed forever. In fact, you will be regarded as all the more vulnerable. This is called the "Pay No Attention to the Man Behind the Curtain" phenomenon.

ORNAMENTATION

As any biologist can tell you, males are the show-offs of the animal world. Peacocks, Siamese fighting fish, lions: Males take a demonstrative, exuberant approach to the Battle of the Sexes. They spread their nuptial plumage, puff up their chests, and engorge their sex glands, aggressively asserting their genetic viability.

The human male is no different. In many parts of the world, our brothers paint their faces, put feathers in their hair, and put on gaudy clothes and jewelry. All in the desperate quest to get laid.

The male's natural inclination to ostentatious frippery represents a difficult dilemma to the modern badass.

BADASS STYLE RULE OF THUMB NO. 1

What chicks dig, adversaries will exploit.
The earring that gives you a pirate's swagger?
It's your opponent's first target in a fierce street-fight—an experienced brawler will tear it off your ear quicker than you can say "Long John Silver." That thick silver chain your lady gave you? Blink, and your adversary's got it wrapped around your trachea.

BADASS STYLE RULE OF THUMB NO. 2

Badasses don't wear jewelry. Not if they want to live.

WATCHES

You're not John Cameron Swayze. Somebody asks you the time, the answer is: "Half past a monkey's ass and a quarter to his balls."

Learn to estimate the time by the position of the sun in the sky; when you get good at it, you'll usually be within half an hour of the actual time. And so what if you're a little late? Make a conscious decision to adopt "Mexican" time. When in doubt, let 'em wait.

RINGS

The only rings the average man should wear are his high school or college ring, his wedding band (known worldwide as "the Ball and Chain"), and a sport's championship ring, say for winning the Super Bowl.

The badass is *not* your average man. The badass should wear nothing on his fingers. Rings interfere with the proper formation of the fist. A misplaced punch while wearing a ring can break your knuckles, yanking you out of the mojo driver's seat and potentially putting you in harm's way. Keep your rings in the top drawer of your bureau at home, next to your socks and condoms.

NOTE: *If you've won a Super Bowl or NBA Championship ring recently, you should have enough dough to hire some bodyguard to carry it around for you.*

EARRINGS/NOSERINGS/PIERCINGS

Leave the body metal to the modern primitives. The badass greets the world the way he came into it—unperforated.

SKIN ART

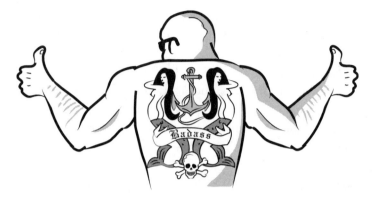

Body art is an integral part of the badass heritage. From Maori warriors to World War II vets, tattoos have decorated badass bodies from Time Immemorial. Like the badass "Walk," a good badass tattoo says, "Trouble coming."

However, in the last 10 years, this artform has blown sky-high in a spray of multicolored ink. Walk down any beach and you'll soon notice that every high school cheerleader, computer geek, and middle-aged housewife has his or her tattoo, from rose-and-thorn anklets to PacMan renderings. Your grandfather's Service souvenir from Honolulu (that battleship sagging and turning blue on his chest) is "Old School." "New School" tattoos depict everything from pixies and Tolkien characters to corporate logos.

A badass birthright has been co-opted. Faced with this welter of skin images, the badass must discriminate. Here's a chart to help you choose acceptable badass body art images.

BADASS TATTOOS

Swallows and bluebirds with banner reading "Mom" in their beaks

Mermaids

Latinas with big butts and perky breasts

Naked or topless women with text: "Man's Ruin"

Dice and cards with text: "Man's Ruin"

Open bottles of booze

Skulls and skeletons

Demonic clowns

Anchors, battleships, and nautical symbols

The Tasmanian Devil

Popeye with a hard-on

DUMBASS TATTOOS

Faeries, Pixies, Nymphs, and Elves (**NOTE:** *This includes all images from* Lord of the Rings)

Corporate logos and product placement

Realistic portraits of the Spice Girls or Britney Spears

Realistic portraits of any Harry Potter character

Your birthday, phone number, or address

Name or image of current girlfriend/wife

Native American kitsch

NOTE: *This includes eagles with wings outspread over desert landscape, grizzlies standing on hindquarters, stags in majestic profile, leaping trout*
Japanese *anime* characters

BADASS HAIR

The rule is: Little or none. The Old School Badasses, World War II and Korean War vets, kept their military service cuts on their return to civilian life. The wartime benefits of short hair were clear: easy to wash and maintain, easy to de-louse and de-tick. And cool under a helmet.

The Old Schoolers soon learned that the short-back-and-sides was useful in non-combat settings as well. Short to no hair means no one's going to grab your curly locks in a fight. Bald is beautiful.

But time marches on and things change. The late twentieth century infusion of bikers and rockers into the ranks of badasses meant that long hair came to be grudgingly accepted. At one time having long hair in certain parts of the US was guaranteed to get you beaten up, or at least hassled. Nowadays, long hair is a standard male tonsorial style. Not the flowing, silky mane of a Fabio, for example, but a stringier, grungier, version—like Kid Rock's.

BADASS FACIAL HAIR

The badass take on facial hair can be summed up in three words: Stubble, stubble, stubble.

From Humphrey Bogart to Clint Eastwood, Bruce Willis to Kurt Russell, the two-day growth look has always been one of the hallmarks of the badass aesthetic. There are several theories to explain this. The historical explanation hearkens back to military veteran style and habits—GIs got used to not shaving when in the field. (Think Bill Mauldin's scruffy heroes, Willie and Joe). Back on the Home Front, not shaving singled the vets out in the button-down, LectraShave '50s as non-conformists. As badasses, peers of bikers, mechanics, pro wrestlers.

The behavioral explanation holds that badasses don't shave because they're too damn busy and obsessed to bother. They're on a mission to save someone or something—you think Duane "Dog" Chapman, world famous bounty hunter, packs a dop kit before he tears out in pursuit of a skip? Then there's a theory that the look derives from the world of boxing—boxers never shave before a bout, their beard taking some of the sting out of their opponent's punches.

Whatever the explanation, the look is here to stay. So the badass challenge is, how to maintain it?

Remember *The Ten Badass Commandments?*

COMMANDMENT 5: Thou shalt never use the stubble head on an electric razor.

Badasses shave only when they have to, i.e., their stubble is becoming a full-fledged beard. Which puts them in an awful quandary—what do you do for that day when you're clean-shaven?

Most badasses use those 12 to 24 hours (depending on your hormones) to catch up on their laundry or bill-paying. Or to go to dinner with your girlfriend's parents. When your beard starts to reassert itself, it's back to badass business.

BADASS HYGIENE

If cleanliness is next to godliness, then badasses rank up there with the archangels. Contrary to popular belief, most badasses maintain a scrupulous regimen of personal hygiene, bathing regularly. The reason? It's as plain as the nose on your face—smelling good gets you laid.

Sweat, the encyclopedia tells us, is part of the human body's cooling mechanism. When the body exerts itself,

waste liquids and salts are released through the pores onto the surface of the skin. Their evaporation serves to lower the body's temperature. It's a marvelously simple bit of chemistry—if you don't think so, check out how dogs cool themselves off. You prefer panting?

Badasses sweat, whether they're scaling a rock face or hurtling a pool table to pound a wise guy. And most women, while they admire badass exertions and acts of physical prowess, are not keen to have your body's waste rubbed all over them. Hence, badasses bathe. Regularly. And thoroughly. A typical badass shower takes three minutes—two minutes to soap up and rinse, topped off by one minute of ice cold deluge. Like rolling in snow after a sauna, it toughens the skin and gets the circulation going.

SOAP

Unscented. Avoid the heavily perfumed brands—skip the Irish Spring unless you're dating a leprechaun.

SHAMPOO

Keep it simple. Any brand that keeps your hair, short or long, from becoming either static-y or an oily, sodden mess. We do not recommend anything with special unguents, moisturizers or conditioners—leave that stuff to the male models and metrosexuals.

DEODORANT

An unfortunate necessity. Like your soap or shampoo, don't let it take over your life. Keep it unscented and unobtrusive. You may be dry, but no chick is gonna get nasty with any guy who smells like "Baby Powder" or "Fresh Lavender." As in all things badass, **less is more.**

SCENTS

Leave it to the French. They took good, old-fashioned "after-shave" (astringents like witch hazel, bay rum or English Leather) and warped it into an entire industry of alcohol-based perfumes and scents (cherishing their *eau de cologne* because it allowed them to avoid the dreaded *eau de bain*). Men who want to can now smell like cinnamon, cloves, patchouli, musk, or any other scent under the sun.

BADASS STYLE RULE OF THUMB NO. 3

Badasses don't wear cologne. On pain of death.

As we have seen, the key to badass success is an overwhelming first impression. Intimidate your opponent at first sight, or risk losing control of the situation to him. And if your opponent's first impression of you is a delicious cloud of citrus spiced with accents of myrhh, you're in deep shit.

So leave the Old Spice and Brut to the college boys. Badasses smell like men. And when they're properly hydrated, with kidneys functioning at 100 percent, men smell just fine.

BADASS ETHNIC TYPES

I have called this principle, by which each slight variation, if useful, is preserved, by the term Natural Selection.
—Charles Darwin, *On the Origin of Species*

The badass, as we've seen, shuns easy categories—he is the essence of unpredictability. So, even as we're pointing out the general characteristics of the genus *badass americanus,* we're aware that there are countless variations on the type.

Like the U.S. of A., the American badass is a whole composed of many parts. Every region, every ethnic group, has its own variation of the badass, from Armenian-American badasses cruising Glendale to Hawaiian badasses barbecuing in Honolulu. Detailing every one of them would require a book of its own. What follows is a field guide to some of the more common badass variations.

AFRICAN-AMERICAN BADASS

HABITAT:	Playgrounds, corners and stoops from Bed–Stuy to Oakland
HAIR:	Retro-fro under hairnet
GEAR:	Carbuncle-size diamond rings, heavy gold and silver chains, precious metal caps on teeth, NBA jerseys, pagers, cells, doo-rags
BOOZE:	Colt 45, Rémy Martin
TEAMS:	Sixers, Steelers, Raiders, UNLV, Miami Hurricanes
TATTOOS:	South Sea abstract, portrait of child relative
TUNES:	50 Cent, Jay-Z, Snoop Dogg, DMX
FLICKS:	*Scarface*

ITALIAN-AMERICAN BADASS

HABITAT:	Pool halls, bars, corners and stoops from Brooklyn to Baltimore
HAIR:	Tony Manero brushcut, the Fade
GEAR:	Gold jewelry, crucifixes
BOOZE:	Olde English 800, Dry Sack
TEAMS:	Jets, Islanders, Steelers, Raiders, Syracuse

TATTOOS: Names of nieces, fiancée

TUNES: Frank Sinatra, KISS, Lou Monte

FLICKS: *The Godfather*

IRISH-AMERICAN BADASS

HABITAT: Bars, corners and stoops from Boston to Chicago

HAIR: Buzz cut under driving cap, the mullet

GEAR: Notre Dame jerseys, crucifixes

BOOZE: Guinness, Jamesons

TEAMS: Celtics, Patriots, Fighting Irish

TATTOOS: Shamrock, Celtics leprechaun

TUNES: Pogues, Frank Patterson

FLICKS: *Gangs of New York*

SOUTHERN/COUNTRY BADASS

HABITAT: Roadhouses, pool halls from Virginia to California

HAIR: Gregg Allman's "Blonde Jesus" locks and beard

GEAR: Trucker cap; skull ring

BOOZE: Budweiser, Jack Daniels

TEAMS: Buccaneers, Cowboys, Spurs

TATTOOS: Confederate flag, Rolling Stones lips

TUNES: Lynyrd Skynyrd, Allman Brothers, Waylon Jennings

FLICKS: *Deliverance*

LATINO BADASS

HABITAT: Bodegas, mercados, corners, and stoops from Harlem to East LA

HAIR: Shaved skull

GEAR: Sunglasses, baggy cut-offs, plaid button down shirts, NFL jersey

BOOZE: Dos XX, Courvoisier

TEAMS: Raiders, Lakers, Kings

TATTOOS: Virgen de Guadalupe

TUNES: Dre; Los Lobos

FLICKS: *American Me*

GREEK-AMERICAN BADASS

HABITAT: Orthodox churches, coffee shops, and stoops from Astoria to Glendale

HAIR: Shaved skull, chest, and back (the "Olympic men's freestyle" look)

GEAR: Gold evil eye pendant, set in lucky horse shoe; gold chains; religious medals; Speedos

BOOZE: Ouzo, Retsina

TEAMS: Nets, Jets, Islanders

TATTOOS: Outline of the Acropolis, image of George Stephanopoulos as toddler

TUNES: Nana Mouskouri; Queen

FLICKS: *Zorba the Greek;* episodes of *Kojak*

THE BADASS WAY TO
USE A ZIPPO

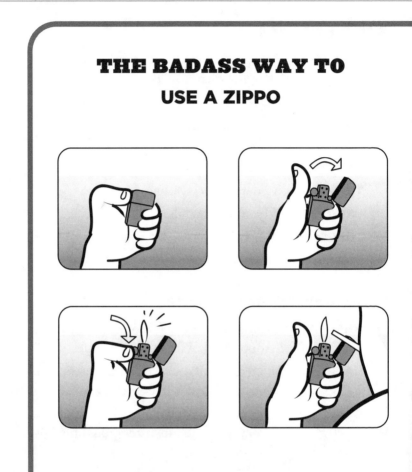

Zippo lighters have been a quintessential badass accessory since WWII. Sleek and palm-sized, the Zippo is hardy, no-frills, and easily serviced. Nicknamed the "GI's best friend," Zippos have been used to signal rescue planes, stop bullets, and placate enraged cargo cult members. The Zippo is the Willey's jeep of incendiary devices.

Over the years, an entire repertoire of tricks have been developed for drawing flame from a Zippo. Our favorite is the one-handed ignite.

1.   With lid shut, grasp lighter in hand, forefinger on hinge, thumb on case opening.

2.   Force lid open with thumb. Swing it back until you hear patented Zippo "click."

3.   Ignite by rubbing thumb against flint wheel.

4.   Touch flame to cigarette/cigar/fuse.

5.   With rapid downward jerk of hand, swing lid shut with satisfying metallic "click."

THE BADASS WAY TO
OPEN A BEER WITHOUT A KEY

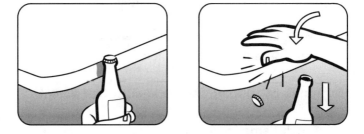

Over the years, multiple methods have been devised for opening beer bottles when no conventional opener (known in the suds trade as a "key" or "church key") is available. Most of these techniques are products of desperation and therefore rife with drawbacks. For example, it is never a good idea to smash the neck of the bottle against a rock or counter—the remaining jagged edges tend to ruin the beer's head. The same goes for using your teeth—it works great in carnival sideshows, but is guaranteed to wreak havoc on your bridgework.

The badass favors just one improvised beer-opening technique: The downward slap.

1.   With one hand, hold bottle upright against aluminum-trimmed or metal-edged countertop, nestling edge of cap against hard edge.

2.   Making sure to keep cap tight against edge, strike top of bottle with meaty part of opposite palm, simultaneously pulling down on bottle with holding hand.

3.   Repeat until cap pops off.

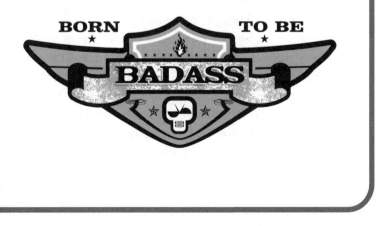

THE BADASS WAY TO
FIGHT A RABID WOLF

It's a scenario straight out of Jack London. Mid-February, Upper Peninsula of Michigan. You're a snowmobiler tinkering with his vehicle. The rest of your party is already up at the roadhouse, downing shots of Jagermeister. It's dead silent in the frosty woods—the only sound the stirrings of an arctic breeze and beating of your heart. It might be peaceful if it weren't so bonechillingly cold.

Suddenly a lone wolf emerges from the frozen underbrush, eyes red, coat thin, spittle flecking its purple maw. It bears all the earmarks of hydrophobia—rabies.

You rise slowly, wrench in hand. Like De Niro in *Cape Fear*, the wolf actually looks away from you, shyly, reluctantly, before it launches itself, fangs bared, at your throat. What do you do?

1. Use that wrench. Chop it hard on the nose.

2. If the wolf chomps down on your arm, shove hard against the back of the beast's jaws. Don't try to pull your arm away. Continue to pound it on the head.

3. Fall to the ground with it, crossing your legs behind its back. Trap it in a leg-lock and squeeze with all your strength.

4. When the wolf attempts to squirm backwards out of your grasp, hit it again and again.

5. Drag vanquished wolf back to the village whistling Prokofiev.

4

CHAPTER FOUR

BADASS CHOW

One of the most fiercely competitive sectors of today's economy is diet plans and weight-loss fads. High-fat, high-protein, low-carb, macrobiotic: There's a theory to match every fat-shedding need.

Ever the iconoclast, the badass shuns diets. Regimented eating is strictly for prisons, boarding schools, and the military. Ever the hunter-gatherer, the badass eats what and when he wants—and what he wants is...

MEAT

Badasses are carnivores. They crave beef, from USDA Prime down to the mysterious catch-all USDA Commercial, Utility, Cutter, and Canner grades. They salivate for pork, from chops to ribs to loins covered with thin sheaths of fat. They crave venison,  boar, goat, moose, whale, and bison. Red, white or purple (ever really look at a slab of venison?), meat is the, well, meat and potatoes of the badass gourmand.

The true badass can savor an aged 18-ounce T-bone steak as well as Spam or potted beef scooped right out of the can. Meat is a badass birthright. If God hadn't intended us to eat meat, why did he make cows so goddamn slow?

THE PLEASURES OF PROCESSED MEATS: NITRITES, NITRITES, NITRITES

The killjoys, insurance underwriters, and attorneys who put the kibosh on badass rituals like unprotected sex, driving with an open container, and riding your hog without a helmet would have us believe that eating processed meats is a form of slow suicide. It's time we told those vegan-weaklings to keep their tort-fearing claws off this vital badass foodstuff.

Badasses savor the wonderful panoply of processed and packaged meats, from Slim Jims to bacon, Vienna sausages canned in brine to cotto salami with its chalky skin intact. This special connection dates back, no doubt, to our hunter-gatherer days, when sun-cured carrion formed the one and only level of the badass food pyramid. (See **Jerky,** below)

You can see how little has changed when you watch a badass stare lustfully at the refrigerator section of his local supermarket. That gleam in his eyes, those moistened lips, are our genome's reaction to processed meat. "Oh I wish I were an Oscar Mayer weiner" indeed.

BADASS FOOD HINT

The eggheads at the nation's research labs warn that increased consumption of processed meats can lead to colon cancer. The deleterious effects of nitrites on your miles of small intestine can be off-set, however, by simultaneously increasing the amount of fiber in your diet. So before you indulge in your daily bacon and olive-loaf bologna fest, we suggest downing a handful of redwood bark mulch (softened with water). It also freshens the breath. Badass problems demand badass solutions.

Barbecue

Badasses crave barbecue—baby back ribs, spare ribs, burnt ends. Some badasses have been know to massage dry rub onto their gums to stave off barbecue withdrawal symptoms. Still others have been caught with fully cooked slabs wrapped in newspaper under their pillows—it makes, they claim, for colorful dreams.

A badass banquet consists of couple of slabs of falling-off-the-bone ribs drenched in barbecue sauce, baked beans (with molasses, smoke, and pit drippings) and a ramekin of marinated coleslaw. Crank up some T-Bone Walker and let the games begin!

Jerky

At the other end of the spectrum, the saltier and more leathery meat becomes, the more badasses relish it. Hence their enduring affection for jerky (and here we're talking beef jerky—no ostrich, fish, or chicken jerky for this badass.)

Jerky dates back, we're told, to the ancient Egyptians—some tomb-raider (whose name has been lost in the mists of time) nibbled on the dead pharaoh's dessicated toe, and culinary history was made. Native Americans dried salted strips of bison and venison in the sun, grinding the dehydrated meat and mixing it with dried fruit and suet to make pemmican. Pioneers trudging across the Great Plains often kept a stash of saltpeter (sodium nitrite) on hand for impromptu food preservation.

Today, there are gadgets galore available to those who want their jerky homemade. Dryers, smokers, special curing powders and bags of fruit wood all make home-drying as easy as building a kit-car.

Then again, you can dispense with all the paraphernalia, toss that roadkill over the clothesline when the Santa Anas are blowing and let Nature do the work. As any badass knows, less is always more.

Hot Dogs and Sausage

Some wisenheimer once quipped that one should never watch legislation or sausage being made (the implication being both processes are stomach-churning.) We say, if the Good Lord hadn't wanted us to eat hot dogs, why'd he give pigs so many barely edible body parts?

So damn the torpedoes. Belly up to that lunch counter and down those lips-and-snouts like a badass. We like ours Chicago style, smothered with raw onion, peppers, and other stuff, though there is a lot to be said for the LA-style, chili-size version and the classic NYC Sabrett with cooked onions and brown mustard. Wash down with a good tap beer or a Yoo-hoo.

THREE BADASS MEAT RECIPES

Nutritious Meals You Can Cook over an Open Flame or Sterno Can

Spam à la Hindenburg

1. Open can of Spam or other potted meat.

2. Slice ½-inch piece of Spam and gingerly remove from can—watch those sharp edges!

3. Fix slice on metal skewer, whittled stick, or car radio antennae.

4. Hold directly over flame. When meat begins to smoke, flip it over.

5. When slice has even crust all over, remove from skewer and eat.

Rotisserie Chicken

1. Rig rotisserie spit out of car radiator fan belt and child's fishing pole.

2. Skewer small (1- to 2-pound) whole chicken— Cornish game hen may be substituted. Brush with marinade of choice.

3. Position rotisserie over flame.

4. Start car engine.

5. Roast for 1 hour, basting meat with drippings every 10 minutes or so.

6. Serve with ketchup (vegetable) and beer (starch) as part of well-balanced meal.

NOTE: *Fully-cooked poultry should have internal temperature of 180°F (82° Celsius).*

Saucisson Auto-da-Fé

1. Skewer sausage links; if links are short enough, a large fork or garden rake may be used.

2. Hold directly over flame. If you need to keep your hands free, wedge handle against firm object.

3. After a moment, sausages should burst into flame. This is fine—this sears the meat, sealing in the juices and flavor. Return skewer to fire—repeat.

4. When sausage is evenly crisp, remove from skewer

5. Enjoy!

VEGETABLES

The badass prefers food that was peripatetic at one point in its existence—if it didn't graze, squirm, swim, slither, or fly, the badass ain't touching it.

Yet a quick glance at the food pyramid hammers home the painful truth—the calorie-fascists at the FDA want us to consume 3 to 5 servings of vegetables every day. Three to 5 servings? You have any idea how many legumes that represents? How many baby squash?

The sad truth is that until some biogeneticist engineers an asparagus that moos, the badass has no choice. He's going to be forced to hold his nose, fight that gag reflex, and eat his veggies.

Chalk it up to the legacy of reform school, prison, or team tables, but badasses favor root vegetables that go squishy with cooking. We're talking the forgotten trio—Rutabaga, Turnip, Kohlrabi. Easy on the gums and tasty when mixed with mashed potatoes or ketchup.

Other sources of vegetable and fruit calories include:

Guacamole	Pepperocini
Ketchup	Salsa
Onion rings	Sauerkraut

Overwhelmed by refrigerator crisper drawers filled with vegetables going limp with neglect? Try this Badass Recipe—a guaranteed crowd pleaser.

Badass Vegetable Toss

1. Dice ½ cup each carrots, celery and onion—set aside. Toss ¾ cup asparagus, 3 or 4 raw beets, 2 parsnips and a handful of Swiss chard into the bowl of a food processor—chop roughly.
2. Combine diced and chopped vegetables in medium-sized mixing bowl. Add 1 clove garlic (peeled and crushed) and mix well.
3. Step out the back door and feed to your pet rabbit.

NOTE: *If you don't have a rabbit, dump it on the ground. Tell your neighbors you're starting a compost heap.*

BADASS GREASY SPOONS

The great smorgasbord that is America offers the badass an infinite variety of choices when it comes to dining establishments. The badass appreciates fine cuisine, but his goal is efficiency and nourishment, not the abstract esthetics of food presentation, minimal portions, and unexpected plate-level marriages of exotic ingredients (also called "biology experiments").

The badass wants chow, and he wants it now. So unless you're itching for a *Three Easy Pieces*-style confrontation with a hipster waiter named Tofer, avoid the eatery-of-the-moment and stick with the tried and true. The places where they know your name... and the fact that you like your scrambled eggs loose and your rye toast dry.

BADASS EATERY ESSENTIALS

A badass eatery should feature some, if not all, of the following:

- A cook with a Lucky Strike dangling from his mouth
- A formica counter running the length of the room
- A men's room with a window opening onto a back alley
- A selection of hot sauces and salsas on each table
- A spinning pie dispenser
- Beef stew and/or menudo
- Booths with squishy leather banquettes
- Clear sight-lines and a view of the street
- Good coffee
- Homemade corned beef hash
- Jukeboxes or phones at each booth
- Laminated menus with frayed edges
- Professional wait staff (no moonlighting actors or musicians) with an average age of 60

Badasses frequent diners near ball parks, stadiums and factories; interstate truck stop coffee shops; casino buffets (we're talking Atlantic City and the older end of the Strip, not Wolfgang Puck's); and burrito, Hawaiian saimin, falafel, and kebab stands.

Tuck your napkin into your collar, roll up your sleeves, drown whatever it is you've ordered with ketchup, and dig in.

Bon Appétit, Badass!

5

BADASS BOOZE

When it comes to booze, A Badass Rule of Thumb applies—Keep It Simple. Badasses take their liquor straight, the way the Good Lord Johnny Walker intended it. Ice is an offense. So are mixers such as soda or tonic. And juices? Are you kidding me? Can you see Lee Van Cleef ordering a Cosmopolitan? Sonny Chiba quaffing a Greyhound? Ordering a fruit drink in a badass bar is grounds for a bitch-slap and the bum's rush.

So it's crucial that the liquor you drink be the very best. Skip the no-name grain alcohol that puts your guts in a knot. Only the best for the badass.

WHAT TO DRINK

WHISKY

Brown liquors rule. From peaty single-malt Scotches to ass-kicking sour mashes, Whiskey is the badass liquor of choice.

Scotch

Blended Scotch whisky (no "e," if you're taking notes) is very popular with the Bridge-playing, blue-hair crowd—the smell of Cutty Sark reminds many a badass of his grandmother. Not an association you want.

Which is why many a badass has discovered the joys of single-malt scotches. Knock back a shot of 25-year old Macallan and you're soon in the mood to put on a kilt, paint your face blue, and kick some English ass.

Bourbon

Over the years, Kentucky bourbon has become linked inextricably to blue grass and bluebloods. Watching some flushed-faced Southern preppy in a button-down shirt and bowtie sipping a mint julep is enough to raise any badass's hackles.

That's why the true badass drinks Tennessee bourbon or sour mash, the rotgut of choice for rockers and bikers.

Think Jimmy Page barfing behind his Marshall stack in *The Song Remains the Same*, or a pack of Hell's Angels toasting each other after they've brained some moped-rider with pool cues and you get a sense of the aura of sour mash.

Jack Daniel's swigged right from the liter bottle is best, but if you've got to use a glass, make it a stubby highball. Straight, no chaser.

TEQUILA

Made from blue agave plants in the Mexican states of Guanajuato, Jalisco, Michoacan, Nayarit and Tamaulipas, tequila comes in four varieties: *blanco, joven abocado, reposado, and añejo*, but the badass sticks with the latter two.

Tequila's been co-opted in the popular imagination by Spring Break college kids getting stupid in TJ on Cuervo shots, but it deserves to be rescued from the forces of darkness. Nothing warms the blood better than a shot of Herradura, followed up by a wedge of lime and some salt licked from a hot chick's cleavage (or off your own hand, if necessary).

MEZCAL

Mezcal is the poor man's tequila. Cruder in taste and effect than tequila, it packs a punch like a mule kick and is said to be a mild hallucinogen.

But even if your bartender seems to be sprouting Day-Glo horns, don't forget the worm that swims at the bottom of many a bottle. Mexicans call it the *gusano*. Its aphro-

VODKA: BADASS?

From the Russian *zhizennia voda* or "water of life." If you've been in a coma for the past few years and haven't noticed, vodka has shoved its way to pole position as the libation of choice for *fashionistas* and hipsters—the shelves of "hot" bars these days groan under the weight of bottles of Grey Goose and a battalion of flavored or "infused" vodkas. Ask for a shot of Rebel Yell and the geek behind the bar'll look at you like you've got two heads.

All this attention has made vodka the most abused of the distilled spirits. Every night, in watering holes across the globe, the lowly vodka is shaken, stirred, strained through ice, whipped in blenders, diluted with juices, liquers and mixers. All in a desperate quest to give it some damn flavor.

If you have to drink vodka, ask for an ice-cold shot of Stoli. Sprinkle some caraway seeds on top, and slam it. Chase with a bite of crisp dill pickle.

disiacal qualities are legendary—some say it'll keep you harder than a hockey stick for three days. *Andale!*

A BADASS BIBLE REMINDER

Any drink that arrives in a stemmed or fluted glass (Martinis, Cosmopolitans) is strictly off-limits for the badass—gotta be something you can wrap your hand around and use as a cudgel in an emergency.

GIN

How the mighty have fallen. From the liquor that built the British Empire, gin has become a tragic also-ran, the stuff you drink when the liquor cabinet has been decimated and it's between the Gordon's and a twenty-year old bottle of Blue Nun.

RUM

Another basic booze that is tarted up and abused ritually by bartenders. Rum benefits by its environment. At a palm-shaded beachfront bar in the tropics, served up by a hottie named Amber wearing a tiny halter top and short shorts, rum (especially the darker brands) goes down easy.

But in less bucolic settings, say a dive bar in Los Angeles, the badass would do well to skip the formalities. Order up a shot of Bacardi 151, ignite it, and down the hatch.

BEER

To the badass, good times *taste like beer*. In our memories, beer is inextricably linked to everything good in life, from empties rolling around the backseat of your high school car to your first sip of a pub-pulled pint of Guinness. With blood and semen, beer forms the Badass Holy Liquid Trinity.

Unfortunately, this sacred essence, this badass Mother's Milk, is being tampered with all too frequently lately. Nowadays, it seems like every Tom, Dick, and Harry Ex-Dot.com CEO has shed his pocket-protector, rolled up his sleeves and gotten into the micro-brewery business. Just troll the refrigerator section of your local supermarket if you need proof of the truly astounding explosion in small-batch brewing that has taken place in the last 10 years. Anyone with a spare two mil has decided he's the next Adolphus Busch.

Few badasses would claim it's an improvement. The baby-brewmeisters adulterate the Holy Suds with fruit (like raspberry), bizarre colorings and additives. They then decant this sludge into oddly-shaped bottles with weird labels (often handpainted by their ADD kids). The Sorcerer's Apprentices have shoved the old Geezer aside and made a total mess of things.

NOTE: *There's some question about where the 40-ounce malt liquors fit in the equation. The Big Daddies like Colt 45 and Olde English 800 have their legions of fans and deserve them—nothing more badass than knocking back a paper-bag wrapped bottle of King Cobra on a muggy August afternoon.*

But you can't order a forty in a bar. Sad, but true.

When in doubt, remember: Keep It Simple. Badasses favor working-class beers ("macrobrews" in the popular parlance), bought right off the shelf—if it's good enough for the men who mine our coal, build our cars, and hammer our steel, it's good enough for us. Take clear stream water, mix it with top quality ingredients, pour it into a bottle with simple lines and a legendary brand-name, and you've got a beer worth drinking.

This is not to say that some of these microbrews might not merit a second sip. If they survive the test of time and are still around, say, 100 years from now, maybe they can share precious shelf space next to the Old Faithfuls. But until then, shove these glorified chemistry experiments to the side and let's get down to some serious brews.

THE BADASS GUIDE TO MACROBREWS

Budweiser. *His Royal Highness, the King of Beers. Long may he reign.*

Leinenkugel's Original Premium Lager. *Chippewa Falls, Wisconsin's finest. Tastes like freedom.*

Yuengling Traditional Lager. *From the country's oldest brewery. Smooth and clear.*

Ballantine Ale. *Our father's and grandfather's beer. Old Reliable.*

Genesee Cream Ale. *A six-pack of this Rochester, New York, beer goes down easy. Buy two.*

Dixie. *Nawlins in a bottle. That's the taste of Louisiana Cypress Wood barrels.*

Rainier Ale. *Packs a whopping 7.2 percent alcohol.*

Mickey's Big Mouth. *Bottles make great containers for 10-penny nails.*

Miller High Life. *The Champagne of Beers. The clear bottle says it all: We're beer, and we're here.*

Pabst Blue Ribbon. *The stuff legends are made of.*

NOTE: *What about Schlitz, some of you may be asking? Or Old Milwaukee? Mississippi Mud Black and Tan? When* you write a book, you can make your own damned list.

WHERE TO DRINK

BADASS WATERING HOLES

In case you haven't noticed, our planet is shrinking rapidly. You can cross the country in a matter of hours. You can buy fresh copies of the *New York Post* in Los Angeles, and find a decent burrito in Manhattan. The eternal verities have been turned inside out. Mostly for the better.

What's for the worse, though, is what's happened to bars:

No Smoking. A drink without a cigarette is like sex without orgasm—unnatural, puritannical, and downright painful.

Not Enough Drinking. In their relentless pursuit of maximum profit and minimum character, bars across the country are neglecting their fundamental duty (serving booze) and installing karaoke machines, holding wet T-shirt contests, and allowing any two-bit auto dealership to sponsor open-mic nights. All in the mad chase after customers... any customers.

In much the way Sin City has reinvented itself as Disneyland North, bars have forgotten their core clientele in their quest for women, college kids, hipsters, and stay-at-home Baby Boomers. They'll stock Zima, put Barry Manilow and Haircut 100 on the jukebox, and hold Mojito recipe contests, all in the name of sales. They'll put doors on the men's room, lay down a dance floor, and even trade in their Simple Green and Comet for those wall-mounted toilet deodorizers that blink in the dark.

It's enough to make a grown man cry. The good news is there are still pockets of sanity out there, where a badass can settle onto a bar stool and sip his drink without being jostled by some jackass in polyester hiphuggers and a too-tight T-shirt reaching for his Red Bull-and-vodka. The dive bars.

Dive bars have a pedigree dating back to the 1800s, when a two-tiered system of drinking establishments held sway. There were the men's clubs, where the robber barons knocked back brandies and talked vertical consolidation, and the saloons, where working men wet their whistles alongside prostitutes, thieves, actors, and the rest of the great unwashed. Prohibition made this secretive world even more secretive; WWII, Korea, and Vietnam filled them with vets drinking to forget. With their sawdust-covered floors and yellowed newspaper clippings tacked up by the manual cash register, dive bars offer a glimpse of an older, rougher era. Which makes them a natural habitat for the badass.

THE BADASS GUIDE TO DIVE BARS

The best dive bars are scratched and defiled, stink of spilled beer and cheap disinfectant, and serve Happy Hour hot dogs no one touches. Here are some of our nation's finest.

Los Angeles: Boardner's
New York City: The Subway Inn

And for those of you in between:

Atlanta: Buckhead Amusement Center
Austin: The Poodle Dog Lounge
Baltimore: Café Tattoo
Chicago: Betty's Blue Star Lounge
Detroit: Post Bar
New Orleans: Lafitte's Blacksmith Shop
Philadelphia: Dirty Frank's Bar

BADASS BAR SKILLS

HOW TO WALK INTO A DIVE BAR

Make no mistake: Dive bars may be the badass' natural turf, but they're strictly hostile territory. Walking into a dive bar can be like walking into the mess hall at San Quentin—you are being watched, weighed up, and judged by a sea of angry eyes searching for an edge.

The key to mastering this gauntlet? Maintain the advantage of mystery.

Dive bars are usually gloomy, smoky places. When you step off the street into a dive bar, particularly during the daylight hours, stop in the doorway. Stand there for a beat or two. Exhale... one, two.

It's the oldest trick in the book, but it still works like a charm. It allows the badass to:

1. Create doubt. Backlit, you look like Trouble. Standing there in silhouette, your expression is unreadable to anyone in the bar. Watch the ripple of uncertainty race across the room: *Who the hell is this?* They can't tell if you're smiling or snarling, and that's right where you want 'em.

2. Size up the situation. The doorway stop allows your eyes to adjust to the low light. Quickly locate the exits, restrooms, juke box, and Happy Hour steam table. Make a mental map of the establishment to call on in case of a brawl.

You should be scoping out the clientele at the same time: how many, where they're sitting, what they're drinking. Potential adversaries come in all shapes and sizes—the true badass can spot a troublemaker by the way he leans on the bar or swigs his Budweiser. *Learn to read Attitude.*

3. Give a nod to the bartender and/or bouncer. If it gets ugly, he could be your new best friend. Let him know *you* know.

ORDERING A DRINK

All right. You're in. It's essential that you continue the show of force you entered the establishment with. The true badass does that without thinking—he can make ordering a drink as intimidating as a Bruce Lee flying kick.

Here's how. With the pause at the door, you've got their attention. Keep the atmosphere right where you want it. Tense. Electric. Like before a dogfight.

1. Approach the bar with strength and confidence. Step up to the nearest stretch of unoccupied bar.

NOTE: *If you have a choice between a spot by a hot girl and a spot by a guy,* pick the guy. *Sounds counter-intuitive, but it communicates to one and all that you came to drink. Sidling up to the hot girl sends the message*: I'm here to get laid. *(That may also be true, but her boyfriend may be the possessive type. Don't stir up a hornet's nest of sexual jealousy before you've even wet your whistle.)*

When you're in position, put your hand face down on the bar top—you want to put it down with enough force to be heard, but not so hard it's a slap. In plain sight. It demonstrates a proprietary air (*"This is my bar"*) and shows your fellow drinkers you're unarmed. When the bartender makes eye-contact, nod slightly.

2. Order clearly, with proper pronunciation. While the bartender stops his business (polishing glasses, watering down bottles of booze) and approaches, scan the shelves for familiar brand names.

NOTE: *Never order a liquor the bar doesn't have—you'll look like an idiot.*

You've found your favorite brand and here he is, sliding a coaster across the bar to you. Give him a mid-paced head nod, look him straight in the eyes and order. Clearly, decisively. Mangling "Laphroaig" or mumbling and then having to repeat an order is an atmosphere killer. *You know what you want. Now make him know it, too.*

Having ordered, too many wannabees just stand there, eyes glistening, looking like a puppy waiting for a treat. Others will even turn and smile nervously at the nearest drinker, as if seeking their approval. *These strategies will result in you getting your ass kicked.*

3. Place your money on the bar while your drink is being poured. Waiting for the bartender to deliver the drink and announce the total makes it look like you're pinching pennies. Five dollars, eight dollars: What difference does it make? *A dive bar is no place to bargain hunt. Cough it up.*

4. Leave your wallet at home. Remember the San Quentin analogy? Would you open your wallet in front of a roomful of rapists and murderers?

A dive bar is no different. Keep your cash in a tight bundle or money clip in your front pants pocket.

Toss a twenty down (It can be a higher denomination, but never lower).

5. Turn and face the room ASAP. Put your street-side elbow on the bar and the heel of your opposite foot on the bar rail.

This posture serves two purposes: It lets you check out the clientele again and test your memory (the guy in the corner is drinking MGD, not Michelob) and it communicates a total control of the situation. It's a posture which says, "I may be a stranger, but I'm still in charge." Again, keep the atmosphere tense. *You are the master of all the mojo in the room.*

6. When your drink comes, don't turn around. The bartender delivers your drink. Your back's turned to him. What do you do? *Nothing. That's his damn job.*

With your back still turned, listen for him taking the bill, making change, then returning with it. Learn to feel when he's moved back to his glass-wiping.

While continuing to face the room, count to two slowly. One Mississippi. Two Mississippi. Now, slowly turn and face your drink.

7. Consider, then drink. Conduct a quick color/volume check—a true badass can discriminate between diluted and undiluted spirits, as well as what constitutes a true eight-plus ounces and what's short.

Take a sip. Roll it over your tongue to test for quality. A good brand should aerate and explode against the palate like the best Bourdeaux.

8. Stand. Don't sit. Only regulars sit. Would you sit down in a lion's den? Stand. Foot up on the bar rail, elbow cocked, hand over the mouth of the glass. Head slightly bowed, as if in thought. Enjoy your drink.

A BADASS BIBLE REMINDER

When your drink arrives, immediately discard any paraphernalia like swizzle sticks, toothpicks, umbrellas, etc. They can block your view and may potentially be used as weapons by adversaries.

DRINKING YOUR DRINK

Every man has his tipping point, that moment when the booze kicks in and starts its sneak attack on your central nervous system. Suddenly, nothing seems to work right. You're weak in the knees, your arms feel like they have lead weights attached to them, and simple statements like "I'll have another" come out all garbled.

You're buzzed. And that's *not* badass. The badass code is as rigorous as *Bushido*—it's an attitude and an ethic that may come naturally to some, may require work by others, but demands constant attention by all. Being a badass is a full time gig, 24/7. Everything—that's right, *everything*—

depends on staying in control of any and all situations. All your hard-earned reflexes, all your training, goes out the window when you've had too many.

The true badass loves to drink, but always stays this side of the Red Zone. Learn to trust your body. Stay within your limits. It's a jungle out there—let your guard down one time, and it may be your last.

Case in point—there's a guy glaring at you from the corner. Disrespect fills the air. What are you going to do?

AVOIDING A BAR FIGHT

That's right—"avoiding." Most bar fights are glorified pissing matches between drunken regulars, guys who haul out long-standing beefs every time they get pie-eyed.

Too often, these regulars are looking for fresh meat to intimidate—it's a way of staying in shape for them. That's the first thing to remember—it's not about you. So, when you feel some bad mojo coming from the dude at the end of the bar with the Cat Diesel hat on, start by not taking it personally.

1. Crack a joke. As any stand-up comedian can tell you, humor is the great tension releaser. A well-delivered joke will get everyone else in the bar on your side. It says to the assembled: "What, me worry?"

Problem is, your nonchalance will probably enrage your adversary. Watch—he'll be the only one who doesn't laugh. He'll make some snide reply, trying to figure out who his allies are. If he's still got numbers, he's going to up the bad mojo ante.

Time to move into action.

2. Go straight at the problem. Approach your adversary. If he's at the bar, leave your spot and stand right behind him.

If he's at a table, walk over to it. In either case, your pace should be steady, your hands loose and lightly clenched at your side in the classic "Gunfighter" stance. (See *The Badass Way to Walk.*)

Give it the badass two-second count, letting the tension in the room mount. This is good. *Remember, you're the unknown quantity.* You'll be able to sense by his body English if he's a candyass playing tough for the crowd or the Real McCoy.

The two seconds up, put your hand on the bar if you're behind him. If he's at a table, sit down opposite him. Both actions show badass balls. Both say "Bring it on."

3. Offer to buy him a drink. That's right. Not "May I buy you a drink?" but "How about another?" A classic ploy in any adversarial situation.

Why? Because the true badass sets the table and lets his adversary serve the main course. You're in the belly of the beast now, the eye of the storm. The moment of decision is here. *It's his move.* What's he going to do?

There are, of course, only two possibilities.

Mr. Wise Ass understands he's up against a professional and accepts the offer. Problem resolved with no blood shed. Or, Mr. Wise Ass blows it big time. He does stupid and makes another derogatory comment. Blood flows.

Assuming it's the latter, it's time to discuss...

WINNING A BAR FIGHT

The Badass Bible is chockful of rules and hints. This is the simplest and most fundamental of them all.

1. Hit first and keep hitting until they drop. He's disrespected you. He's rejected your peace-making gesture.

Clearly, he has what Sigmund Freud called a "death wish." Time to oblige him.

As in any violent encounter, everything and anything is a weapon for the badass. Tables, chairs, ashtrays, highballs, fists, the top of your head, elbows, steel-toed boots, other patrons—Wise Ass has just ordered a world of hurt on himself. And you're the UPS man.

2. Know when to stop. The severity of your response should be determined by the severity of the threat. When your opponent is vanquished, **STOP**. Whether it's a short sharp shock or a full-bore, chair-smashing donnybrook, it's all over when Wise Ass cries "Uncle."

The good news is, W.A.'s out of commission for a while. The bad news is, your opportunity for a relaxing drink is shot. Time to go.

3. Finish your drink. If it survived the fracas, down it. Hell, you paid for it. There's probably been damage to the bar's physical plant. Commiserate with the bartender. Toss a twenty on the bar—chances are he'll decline it. Take a last look over at your downed opponent and...

4. Walk out. The way you came in. Like Master of the Universe. Now *that's* badass.

THE FINER POINTS OF HITTING

As any boxer can tell you, hitting an adversary in the head with your closed fist is like hammering a nail with a baby chick—it's a given that lots of tiny bones are going to get crunched.

The badass strikes with:

- the side of his fist (*hammer fist*)
- the meaty side of the palm (*heel palm*)
- the stiff tips of fingers (*finger rake/jab*)
- the cupped hand (*ear slap*)
- the top of the head (*head butt*)
- the elbow (*elbow strike*)
- the knee (*knee strike*)

The badass may be slow to anger, but he is ruthless in counterattack. Your targets are anywhere your opponent is vulnerable. Keep it simple, efficient, and quick.

Example One
Wise Ass gets up. Don't wait to see if he's heading for the bathroom or wants to dance. In rapid succession, you respond with:

- finger jab to his esophagus
- front kick to his stomach/groin

when he's doubled over, crack him with an elbow strike under the chin. He'll have plenty of time to reorganize his priorities in La-La Land.

Example Two

Wise Ass grabs you from behind. You respond with:
- elbow strike under the chin
- heel palm to drive his head even farther back
- knee strike to the groin for good measure

He'll apologize in a falsetto.

6

BADASS WHEELS

You are what you drive.

These days, nearly every demographic group has its own distinctive set of wheels. Take a gander around any parking lot in America and you'll see what we mean. Aging hippies and Silicon Valley types drive electric cars, urban hipsters drive pastel Volkswagen Bugs or Mini-Coopers, and soccer moms drive mini-vans. Working men drive 4x4s, aspiring starlets K-cars with out-of-state plates, and rappers, Escalades. Tell us your sex, profession, income bracket and ethnic background and we can tell you what kind of car you drive.

Badasses drive muscle cars.

The heyday of the muscle car was brief but intense. It's hard to imagine in this era of crippling fuel efficiency standards and alternative-fuel burning hybrid cars, but for about a decade starting in the early '60s, high-performance muscle cars ruled the streets. For that brief, shining moment, American car manufacturers were locked in a high-tech arms race measured in speed-to-weight ratios... and drivers won. Year after year, Chevrolet, Dodge, Ford and Pontiac cranked out some of the meanest machines this side of the drag strip.

That is, until sky-high insurance rates and new federal emissions standards brought production of these "beautiful brutes" to an end. Ten-plus years of mag shreddin', ear-splittin', teeth-chatterin' badass wheels. It was a hell of a badass ride.

BADASS CLASSIC MUSCLE CARS

1962 Chevrolet Bel Air 409. "Bubble-top" two-door hardtop. 409-cid, 409-hp engine. Toss in a close-ratio four-speed manual transmission and look out. As the Beach Boys sang, "She's so fine, my 409."

1966 Chevrolet Chevy II Nova SS. A "factory hot rod." 327-cid, 350-hp V8 engine. Zero to 60 in just over seven seconds. Breath-taking.

1970 Chevrolet Chevelle SS 454. 454-cid big block engine. A killer.

1968 Dodge R/T Charger Fastback. Drop in the optional 426-cid, 425-hp Hemi V-8 and look out.

1963 Ford Galaxie Lightweight. 427-cid, V-8 engine. White exterior, red interior. Devilish.

1965 Ford Mustang GT. A legend in its own time.

1966 Ford Fairlane GTA. 390-cid, 335-hp V-8. It's lean and mean.

1966 Oldsmobile 4-4-2. "Four-barrel carburetion; 4-On-The-Floor; 2-Dual Exhausts." You're lucky if you have time to get out of the way.

1969 Plymouth Road Runner. Sporting a 440 "Six Pack." Horn sounded like the Warner Bros. cartoon character: "Beep beep."

1967 Pontiac GTO. Mid-size body, big block engine, affordably priced: the classic muscle car.

BADASS NEW POWER RIDES

So you don't own one of these classic beasts. Doesn't mean you've got to walk, or resort to driving a Honda Element (even hitching a ride in one of those godawful contraptions makes your badass status suspect).

Nowadays, the badass has a full range of possibilities when it comes to cars with *cojones*. We've been lucky to be born into a time when cars can be both environmentally-friendly and kick-ass. Match up any of these rides against a classic muscle car....

2004 Dodge Viper SRT-10. Low, sleek, like a snake's head on wheels. Its 8.3-liter V-10 (that's right, V-10) cranks out 500 hp. Eat my dust.

2004 Chevrolet Corvette Z06. Celebrating over 50 years of automotive excellence. The LS6 V-8 in this monster generates 405 hp.

2004 Mitsubishi Lancer Evolution. The new kid on the block, favorite of SoCal street racers. Forget the "rice burner" rap—give the Lancer a straightaway and this turbocharged monster with the low-profile spoiler will tear it up.

Okay, so you want some size to go with your power. These days, when even premium rides like the Caddy have shrunk to the size of a 1970's Datsun two-door, who can blame you for wanting some leg-room to spread out? SUV, you say? SUVs are just Volvos on steroids. For the badass who wants to dominate the road, there's only one vehicle—

2004 Hummer H1. Remember the kid's book about the bear hunt? "We can't go *over* it. We can't go *under* it. Oh

no! We've got to go *through* it." The H1 can go through a brick wall.

Check out these specs: 184.5 inches long. At 86.5 inches wide and 77 inches high (minus roof rack), this behemoth is as wide as it is tall. Has a water-fording (that's right) depth of 30 inches. Turbocharged diesel engine. It's like driving a small house. Just remember to hang the "Wide Load" sign out back.

BADASS CAR FLICKS

Along with women-in-prison and out-of-control giant creature flicks, hot rod movies are a perennial mainstay of American B-movies. Some have suggested they're a curious updating of old-style Westerns, with gas-guzzling roadsters substituted for horses. Or that they're gladiator movies on wheels. (Yeah, and the *Wizard of Oz* is really about American isolationism on the eve of World War II.)

All we know is, some of the best B-movies of the '70s were hot rodders, and the overwhelming success of today's *Fast and Furious* series is proof that the brand is still going strong. Something about a high-powered set of wheels and an empty stretch of road just seems to bring out the badass best in many a filmmaker.

Two-Lane Blacktop (Dir: Monte Hellman, 1971). Singer/songwriter James Taylor and Beach Boy Dennis Wilson race their '55 gray primer Chevy cross-country against Warren Oates in his 1970 Pontiac GTO. Hellman gets great understated performances out of his musician actors, and Oates is at his best as a bullshit artist continually reinventing himself. All three motorheads get sideswiped by the one thing they can't rev up—a woman. Great drag racing footage.

Vanishing Point (Dir: Richard C. Sarafian, 1971). Car-deliverer Barry Newman trics to outrun his traumatic past (and a convoy of cops) in a 1970 Dodge Challenger R/T, egged on by blind DJ Super Soul (Cleavon Little). Sarafian pushes the existentialist implications of the man/car/desert nexus to the max, with the Challenger kicking up dust as it speeds across what looks like the surface of the Moon. Invaluable funk score.

Gone in 60 Seconds (Dir: H.B. Halicki, 1974). Writer/director/producer/actor Halicki and his group of car thieves (all in identical gray wigs and mirror sunglasses) must steal 48 cars ASAP. There are gadgets galore in this gearhead wet-dream. Infamous for its 40 minute car chase. Only known feature film with a Ford Mustang Mach 1 listed as a star.

Bullitt (Dir: Peter Yates, 1968). Steve McQueen exudes badass cool as Frank Bullitt, a San Francisco detective who smells a political cover-up in a mob murder. The high speed chase through Baghdad-by-the-Bay between McQueen's fastback Mustang GT and the hitmen's '68 Charger is hands-down the best car chase in film history.

Ronin (Dir: John Frankenheimer, 1998). Frankenheimer resuscitates the classic car chase, with freelance intelligence agent De Niro eluding his adversaries in a white-knuckle ride across Paris, highlighted by De Niro driving against traffic through a tunnel during what looks like rush hour.

Mad Max and *Mad Max 2: The Road Warrior* (Dir: George Miller 1979, 1981). An essential double-feature. Mel Gibson stars as Max, ex-cop roaming the Australian outback of the near-future, a high octane wilderness filled with murderous gearhead gangs and survivalists. Miller captures the simplicity and grittiness of Roger Corman-era B-movies perfectly, giving the whole package a Down-Under exoticism. Must-see DVDs.

The French Connection (Dir: William Friedkin, 1971). Friedkin keeps it simple—Gene Hackman's Popeye Doyle, porkpie hat askew, commandeers a car and tears ass under an elevated subway train. Brilliantly shot and cut, it's a heartstopping interlude in this classic '70s anti-hero flick. Up there with *Bullitt* as one of the very best.

The Fast and the Furious (Dir: Rob Cohen, 2001). High-stakes drag racing on the streets of suburban Southern California. Vin Diesel's smoldering performance put him on the Hollywood map.

The Gumball Rally (Dir: Chuck Bail, 1976). So who said car flicks have to be dead serious? A rollicking cross-country race filled with cameos and great stunts.

Deathrace 2000 (Dir: Paul Bartel, 1975). Karl Marx once opined that history repeats itself, first as tragedy, then as comedy. In a matter of years, the existential angst of

Vanishing Point was being played for laughs—Paul Bartel (*Eating Raoul*) parodizes the road race as a gladiatorial deathsport. The laughs don't obscure the high-performance vehicles he crams into every frame.

BADASS BIKES

No, we don't mean those things you pedal. We're talking hardcore two-wheel road rockets here. Raw power. From pre-Hinkley Triumphs to the should-be-illegal power of the Kawasaki Ninjas, the motorcycle is always a vehicle of choice for the badass. Here are the fastest and meanest classics mixed with state-of-the-art road warriors.

Kawasaki ZX-11 Ninja. Turbocharge it with nitrous oxide fuel injection and hold on tight.

Honda CBR 1100XX. A monster at 492 pounds, it sports a gigantic 1137cc engine.

Triumph Bonneville. A classic. Defined "motorcycle" for generations.

Yamaha YZF-R1. 998cc, 20-valve engine. Recalls the innovation of the '87 FZR 1000.

Suzuki Hayabusa 1300. Massive 1299cc engine.

1971 BSA 550. Oldie but goodie.

Harley Davidson FXDR Dyna Glide Low Rider. Low-slung seat, raked-out front fork. Carries 1450cc Twin Cam 88.

Indian Chief. Biggest of the group. 1638cc V Twin. If it's good enough for the Terminator, it's good enough for you.

Buell Firebolt XB9R. Features Erik Buell's innovative all-aluminum frame, which encompasses the bike's fuel tank. All in the quest for speed.

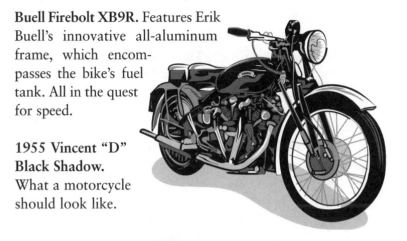

1955 Vincent "D" Black Shadow. What a motorcycle should look like.

BADASS DRIVING SKILLS

HOW TO DRIVE AND SURVIVE

Imagine a ton of metal and glass hurtling by you at speeds of up to 100 miles per hour. Now, multiply that by several thousand, and you've got a picture of a typical American big-city highway at rush hour. A fast-flowing, lethal river of steel projectiles. The physics alone are terrifying.

Now put a numbskull chatting on his cell phone behind the wheel, or a housewife scolding her kids, and you've got a recipe for disaster. Last year, the Department of Transportation recorded more than 40,000 fatalities out of an estimated six million traffic accidents. You've got to do everything you can to avoid being one of them.

The bad news is, you're not going to have a lot of help. Most people have no right to be behind the wheel of anything faster than a riding mower. (**NOTE:** *These are the same Joe Six-Packs who should not be allowed to operate* *power tools.*) But they keep cranking out those licenses and clogging our streets with the transportationally-challenged.

There are animal, vegetable, and mineral hazards as well. Deer, moose, armadillos, crabs (yes, crabs) will all scamper into your headlights from time to time, mistaking your badass vehicle for food or a potential mating partner. Don't be Cupid's victim. If a love-sick Bambi wanders into your path on a dark stretch of country road, don't swerve suddenly or jerk the wheel—why run the risk of fishtailing or rolling over?

Don't avoid... aim. Clip the bastard, minimizing damage to your prize vehicle, then go back and finish it off with a finger-jab between its beady eyes. Put the "kill" back in "roadkill."

Equally lethal are the obstacles that don't have pulses: fallen trees, rock slides, avalanches, flash floods. Any one of these can ruin your tranny but good. Be prepared— know your route and learn to spot the early-warning signs of avalanche or flash-flood danger. These include new snow, thaw conditions, snowballs rolling downhill, and rapidly rising water levels in local streams and rivers.

Finally, beware the many man-made, infra-structural hazards out there. Our network of roads and highways are in dire need of repair and maintenance. In the outer boroughs of New York, there are potholes large enough to swallow your car whole. When it rains in Southern California, the road surfaces grow slick with months of leaked engine oil—before you know it, your car will be hydroplaning across lanes like an Air Hockey puck.

It's a mess out there—a life-threatening mess. The badass has but one choice—control the situation. In a word: You've got to drive **Defensively.**

4 SIMPLE RULES THAT JUST MIGHT SAVE YOUR LIFE

1. Maintain your vehicle. Driver's Ed 101. Keep your vehicle road-worthy with tune ups and regular inspections. This includes boring but life-preserving equipment like wipers, de-frosters, head and taillights. If you can't see the move the bonehead in the Econline van with the blackened windows is about to pull, how can you possibly avoid it?

2. Maintain yourself. Again, Driver's Ed basic curriculum. Never drive impaired. The badass shuns inebriation. It's an intolerable, and usually dangerous, loss of control. Sleep in your car if you have to, but badasses do not walk, ride or drive under the influence.

This rule goes beyond booze, pills, and powders. Anything that interferes with your total concentration on the road and the cars around you is a hazard to be avoided—this includes business calls, love sickness, sunstroke, receiving handjobs or blowjobs—all verboten. Driving is a deathsport—it requires total commitment.

3. Assume your fellow driver intends to kill you. Anticipate stupidity...or worse. Start from the premise that your fellow driver's sole purpose for being on the road today is to sideswipe, rear-end, cut off, encroach upon, or otherwise assault you. Whether it's the little old lady from Pasadena or some hopped-up construction worker in a tricked-out Ford Bronco, they are out to cause you bodily harm.

The eighteenth-century primer, *The Book of the Samurai,* is useful in this regard.

"Meditation on inevitable death should be performed daily. Every day when one's body and mind are at peace, one should meditate upon being ripped apart by arrows, rifles, spears and swords, being carried away by surging waves, being thrown into the midst of a great fire, being struck by lightning, being shaken to death by a great earthquake, falling from thousand-foot cliffs, dying of disease or committing seppuku at the death of one's master. And every day without fail one should consider himself as dead."

The badass must be able to recognize death, whether it takes the form of a big rig that's lost its brakes, or a bimbette in a Miata who's got her hands off the wheel as she roots around under her seat for her Shakira CD. Like the knight in Ingmar Bergman's classic, *The Seventh Seal*, when the badass recognizes Death, he can start to play with it.

4. Plan an escape route. Expect adversity. If Car A cuts me off, and Car B is bearing down on me in the number 3 lane, I'll brake, downshift, and slip in behind the Navigator with the "Child On Board" sign. Details. Commit them to memory and they just might save your life.

"But how?" you ask. "How can I possibly know what my fellow driver is going to do?" It's simple. You're telepathic. Now, channel sheer stupidity. And remember: Whatever you come up with is still a best-case scenario.

BADASS DRIVING SCHOOLS

Luckily, there are a growing number of professional driving schools across the country, geared towards offering you the tools you'll need to drive and survive.

Bobby Ore Motorsports High Performance Driver Training. Ore offers lessons in steering skills, skid control, and crash avoidance, as well as stunt driving techniques and counter-terrorist tactics. Essential skills for your daily commute.

Keith Code's California Superbike School. Code maintains there are at least 11 elements to successful cornering on a high-performance motorcycle. He teaches them all. Hard-core racers flock to his school, but the skills he imparts are equally useful in dodging the teenager in the Neon who's drifting into your lane.

THE BADASS WAY TO

START A FIRE USING A CAR BATTERY

No matches. Somebody yanked the cigarette lighter out to recharge their cell phone and neglected to put it back. Night's coming on and the temperature's plummeting.

You need to start a fire. Fast. You could:

• Carve a block of ice into a concave lens and use it like a magnifying glass.

No ice.

• Mix potassium permanganate crystals and sugar and grind with a firebow.

No sugar. No potassium permanganate (whatever that is). *No firebow*.

"Panic" is not in the badass thesaurus. A roaring fire is just four easy steps away:

1. Gather some very dry kindling and tinder. Keep it close—only an idiot starts a fire without adequate fuel.

2. Wrap a handkerchief with a coiled length of wire and wet with a small amount of gasoline. (Too much and you're bound to lose your eyebrows when it flares up.)

3. Open the hood and expose the engine. Protect everything but the battery using floor mats, coats, clothes—you want to prevent any gas vapor from seeping out.

4. Attach two lengths of barbed wire to the battery terminals and loop them away from the car. (You can also use two wrenches.) Touch the ends together to create a spark. Capture the spark with your gas-soaked handkerchief. Touch your impromptu torch to the pile of tinder. Blow.

Sounds easy, doesn't it? Well, it ain't. Chances are you'll drain your battery and/or burn your hands. Your frustration should heat you up. Option two? Wrap yourself in a warm blonde to get the circulation moving.

THE BADASS WAY TO
OPERATE ON YOURSELF

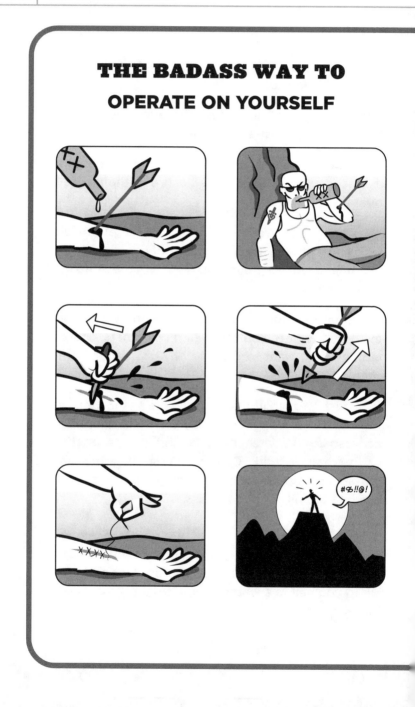

Remember the news story about Aron Ralston, the take-no-prisoners rock climber? His arm pinned and crushed by a massive boulder, strength ebbing after five days in the open, with no sign of help on the horizon (hell, he couldn't even see the horizon), Ralston calmly pulled out a pocketknife and cut his arm off at the elbow. Operation completed, he tied off the severed end, rappelled to the canyon floor and walked out to find help. Now that's badass.

As Aron could tell you, operating on yourself is an exercise in inverse proportions—the clearer your head, the better the work, but the greater the pain. Too much pain and you pass out, leaving the operation incomplete. On the other hand, using alcohol or drugs will numb the pain, but cloud your faculties and possibly jeopardize the operation.

What's a badass to do?

1. Prepare wound and instruments. Sterilize the wound and surrounding area with antiseptic swab. If swab is unavailable, use high proof alcohol or your own urine. Sterilize instruments (scalpel, pocket knife, butter knife) by dipping in antiseptic, booze, or urine. Save a sip of booze for yourself. Discard urine.

2. Prepare ye. Take a swig of booze and analyze the situation. Take another swig. That's enough.

3. Make the incision. Whether removing an enemy bullet or a really bad splinter, make the incision as clean as possible. Scars make great conversation starters, but chicks find jagged, disfiguring gashes a turn-off.

4. Extract foreign body. Work quickly. The endorphins should be spilling into your blood stream right about now, as your most primitive reptile brain strains to convince itself that you can survive this ordeal.

Locate offending object (bullet, nail from nail gun, etc.) and pry free of flesh.

5. Take another swig.

6. Douse wound with an antiseptic and close it with needle and thread, knitting needle and yarn, or a three-penny nail and shoelace

7. Howl with pent-up agony.

7

BADASS GIGS

Remember the Kurosawa flick *The Seven Samurai*? After the breakdown of feudal hierarchical order, bandits roamed the countryside harassing the peasantry. Samurai were badass guns (or swords) for hire, freelance specialists in medieval chopsocky. They were treated by the populace with respect and awe—in return for the samurai's martial arts skills and defensive services, the peasants would turn over their rice and their daughters. Tits for tat, as it were.

For a badass, life was good.

Nowadays, many badasses find themselves stuck in dead-end gigs that insult their intelligence and abilities. You can blame it on wrong-headed supply side economics or the outsourcing of crucial manufacturing jobs, but the typical badass often finds himself working a job any reasonably bright 9th grader could handle. It's like squeezing Clint Eastwood into a Chuck E. Cheese uniform and asking him to man the deep-fryer.

It'd be funny if it weren't so pathetic.

The good news is, you can always quit. Here are some jobs better fit for badass bravado. They require sweat, muscle, and balls the size of watermelons.

BOUNTY HUNTER

From Steve McQueen's film portrayal of Wyoming bounty hunter Tom Horn to the south-of-the-border antics of Duane "Dog" Chapman, bounty hunters have always captured the popular imagination. They're the big game hunters of the law enforcement world, the men who track other men for a living.

Yet even in this dangerous demi-monde of skips, escapees, and Most Wanteds, political correctness has reared its pathetic little head. "Bounty hunter" you say? You must mean "bail enforcement agent." That bloodless

neologism doesn't change what these guys do—track down and collar baddies, the "most dangerous game." It's what they live for. As amateur poet "Dog" Chapman puts it,
"Born on a mountain, raised in a cave,
Arresting fugitives is all I crave."

REPO MAN

Otherwise known as stealing cars for a living. Only semi-legitimate in the eyes of the Law. As a heart-pounding, adrenaline-pumping good time, second only to getting a lap dance from Jenna Jameson. *You* may know you're authorized by some financing company to go-jack and throw your hooks onto Joe Six-Pack's new Infiniti, but chances are *Joe* doesn't—and he's standing there wearing nothing but a sawed-off shotgun and a bad attitude.

Every repo is a game of Russian roulette... with all but one of the chambers loaded.

SMOKE JUMPER

Ready to parachute from 2,000 feet out of a Twin Otter onto blazing, heavily-timbered terrain? You'll need to pass a Navy SEALs-type minimum fitness test and clock in at least a year of wildland fire experience before you do. That'll just earn you the right to hump a 100-pound pack up and down smoldering ravines and knock down forest fires using little more than brains, guts, and an axe.

Maybe that job flipping burgers wasn't so bad after all—if something's gotta fry, might as well not be you.

OFFSHORE OIL-RIG WORKER

Fourteen days afloat, pounded mercilessly by the raging sea. The same mess hall day in and day out, the same faces and bad jokes. Sea-sickness, homesickness, an

uncontrollable horniness that has to wait for your next 21-day furlough...

Captain Stubing's journal entry for an episode of the *Love Boat*? In fact, it's a description of life on an off-shore oil rig. Boring into the earth's core for ever-elusive pockets of crude, the operative word being "boring." Backbreaking, muscle-numbing work.

And no shuffleboard.

DEEP-SEA SALVAGE DIVER

The part of the "world beneath the sea" Jacques Cousteau never bothered to tell us about.

The laughs are few and far between as you try to survive (let alone operate) in an alien environment (air pressure so severe it can crush a basketball to the size of a peanut) while breathing mixed gases out of a hose. Makes outer space feel downright welcoming. Your only company: silt, buried transatlantic cables, and a stray halibut.

STOCK CAR RACER

The NASCAR promos would have you believe being a racer is as glamorous as being, say, a champion polo player... well, it ain't. Motels, greasy spoons, flat-towing your rig from race to race like Sisyphus and his rock—too often, racing feels like real work. And for what? Weeks of training and preparation leading up to an explosion of sound, fury, and excitement. And it's over before you know it.

Sounds like your last date, doesn't it?

TEST PILOT

Why should Chuck Yeager have all the fun? Go to the National Test Pilots School in the Mojave desert and learn how to put a state-of-the-art aircraft into a death spiral. Watch the engineers and designers on the ground blanch and lose their collective lunches as you put their multi-million-dollar baby through its paces. Buzz the tower just for the hell of it.

BULL RIDER

Strap yourself onto 1,800 pounds of enraged beef and have someone give the bull's flank strap a hard yank. Your kidneys will be up around your earlobes before you can say "Whoa, Ferdinand." Wait—there's more. You have to hold on to your roughstock rocket with one hand (other hand can't touch the bull) for eight seconds. Oh, and try not to get tossed, horned, or stomped.

Tough on the innards and testicles, but chicks dig that bow-legged walk.

ALLIGATOR WRESTLER

It's been said that there are 80 good reasons not to mess with an alligator—40 top teeth and 40 bottom.

No longer the sole province of Seminole Indians performing for sun-burned Snowbirds, 'gator wrestling has gone mainstream (thanks, Steve Irwin). You'll have to master the nose-touch and jaw slam and be willing to lose a finger or lower leg, but all's fair in love and tourist entertainment. So don your safari outfit, get down there in the muck and mire and teach Wally Gator the lesson of his miserable prehistoric life.

NEW YORK CITY BUS DRIVER

Keep several tons of rolling stock on schedule while being harassed by gangbangers, schizophrenics, and little old ladies demanding to be dropped off in the middle of the block. You can't listen to music, use your cell phone, or take unplanned bathroom breaks.

Now *that's* badass.

CHAPTER EIGHT

BADASS KICKS

All work and no play makes Jack a dull boy.
—Trad.

What, you ask, qualifies as badass entertainment? Axe-throwing? Cockfighting? Midget-tossing? Tattooing yourself with a rusty nail and some India ink?

Well, all this... and more. Badasses are just like you and me... only more so. They like to watch movies, listen to music, read a good book every once in a while, go out and catch a live show. Their enjoyment of everyday cultural pursuits is limited only by their general impatience with the antics of the hoi polloi, a.k.a. your everyday, run-of-the-mill jackass. Oh, and their fierce tempers. And the fact that Smartass over there in the corner is bobbing his head in an annoying manner. And Douchebag just bumped my arm and spilled some of my beer....

Occasionally, even the hardest-core badass needs to let his hair down (as it were: See **Badass Hair**) and cut loose. For him, we've devised the following guide to badass entertainment.

BADASS FLICKS

Second only to war, films have had the greatest impact in defining and promoting the essence of *badass*. Hollywood loves badasses. From yesterday's steely-eyed cowboy star William S. Hart to today's Vin Diesel, the badass has always been one of the Silver Screen's finest obsessions and greatest draws.

Which makes choosing the top badass flicks as tough as, say, picking which Rockette you want to take home for private high-kicking lessons. It's an embarrassment of riches, as they say. With that caveat, here are some of our favorites, in no particular order.

The Dirty Dozen (Dir: Robert Aldrich, 1967). Lee Marvin, Ernest Borgnine, Jim Brown, John Cassavetes, Robert Ryan, Charles Bronson... A veritable Who's Who of American Badasses shed their lyin', thievin', whorin' ways to take on the Hun. Not to be missed.

Dirty Harry (Dir: Don Siegel, 1972). Clint Eastwood goes iconic as Harry Callahan, a hard-as-nails SF detective who bucks the system and pursues serial killer Scorpio on his own.

Eastwood exudes badass cool—watch for the bank robbing scene in which Eastwood, leg perforated with shotgun pellets, still manages to finish the hot dog he's eating.

Fascinating encapsulation of Vietnam-era law-and-order debate. Also features unforgettable Lalo Schiffrin score.

Enter the Dragon (Dir: Robert Clouse, 1973). Top-of-the-line chopsocky as Bruce Lee (in his last complete film role) travels to the island fortress of steel-clawed villain Han to infiltrate a martial arts tournament.

Lee is a wire-tight mass of muscle, mixing fury, humor and impossible elegance with each blow. His slow-boil response to being wounded (he touches and tastes his own blood, then comes unglued) is the quintessence of *badass*. Also stars '70s martial arts phenom Jim Kelly and film and TV stalwart John Saxon.

The Killers (Dir: Don Siegel, 1964). Like Robert Siodmak's 1946 classic of the same name, Siegel's *Killers* is based on a Hemingway's short story about a rub-out.

Lee Marvin and Clu Gulager are hitmen puzzling out why someone wants race driver Johnny North (John Cassavetes) dead—their curiosity piqued, of course, after they've already wasted him. The trail leads back to head honcho Ronald Reagan and she-devil Angie Dickinson—after dispatching Reagan, Marvin replies to Angie's pleas for mercy with a weary, "Lady, I haven't got the time." Blam.

The Wild Bunch (Dir: Sam Peckinpah, 1969). William Holden, Ernest Borgnine, Robert Ryan, Edmond O'Brien, Warren Oates, Ben Johnson and more in Peckinpah's operatic oater about the last heist by a group of aging outlaws. A Romantic paean to outdated ethics, impossible odds, and the steady, crushing march of Time.

Peckinpah's slow-motion ballets of blood set an unimpeachable standard today's action filmmakers still cannot improve on. Watch for the brutal shoot-out with the Mexican army, complete with Gatling gun.

Scarface (Dir: Brian De Palma, 1983). Al Pacino is Tony Montana, Cuban refugee and crime-lord on the make in this Oliver Stone-penned masterpiece. Almost three hours of blood, sweat, and tears, with a final shoot-out that ranks up there as a paradigm-shifting best. A contemporary classic, beloved by gangsta rappers, energy executives, and effete intellectuals.

Hardboiled (Dir: John Woo, 1992). Chow Yun-Fat is the essence of cool as Tequila, a Hong Kong cop caught in the middle of a gun-running gang war. The slow-motion fusillades (check out the furious shoot-out in the hospital) of Woo's Hong Kong flicks were a powerful influence on the work of Quentin Tarantino and others—his Hollywood flicks, however, have been far less ground-breaking.

Point Blank (Dir: John Boorman, 1967). Lee Marvin brings a weary, laconic nobility to his role as Walker, seeking righteous vengeance after being shot and left for dead by his unfaithful wife and his best friend. Director Boorman makes the most of this existentialist trope: The portrait of a man with nothing to lose driven to seek an impossible revenge.

Billy Jack (Dir: Tom Laughlin, 1971). Writer/director Tom Laughlin stars as Billy Jack, a half-breed ex-Green Beret pacifist with one of the worst tempers this side of the Tasmanian devil. Sort of an updated *Shane*—except this Shane sports a big black hat, speaks in an affectless mumble, and takes out his adversaries with modified martial arts moves.

XXX (Dir: Rob Cohen, 2002). Badass-of-the-moment Vin Diesel infiltrates Eastern European crime syndicate using his biceps, wits and a panoply of X-treme gadgets. Too much tongue-in-cheek, second-rate James Bond pyrotechnics, but there is enough badass muscle in there to rate.

The Terminator (Dir: James Cameron, 1984). With each sequel, the *Terminator* franchise has grown progressively more bloated. The first installment, however, is exactly as it should be—lean, mean, with the no-nonsense directness of a great comic book.

Schwarzenegger's career-making performance as a murderous cyborg plays to all his strengths: a relentless physicality, a brutal single-mindedness and a blatant disregard for the subtleties of the English language.

Get Carter (Dir: Mike Hodges, 1970). A brittle Michael Caine is Carter, a London Mob enforcer who travels to his grimy Midlands hometown, Newcastle, to bury his brother, stumbling over the workings of a seedy regional underworld in the process. This original blows the Stallone remake out of the water with its grit, its documentary realism, and the sheer power of Caine's anguished character.

The Seven Samurai (Dir: Akira Kurosawa 1954). A *Dirty Dozen* in kimonos. Kurosawa gathers his elements slowly, allowing the individual quirks of his band of heroes to sink in. Shakespearean in scope, thoroughly modern in detail, *Samurai* is a classic depiction of men and a mission.

The Yakuza (Dir: Sydney Pollack, 1975). A bone-weary Robert Mitchum travels to old stomping-ground Japan to search for kidnapped daughter of pal Brian Keith, leading him into the tattooed clutches of the *yakuza* or Japanese Mob. Frustrated by duplicity and ritual, Mitchum's slow-burn is a marvel to watch—all his fury explodes in a no-holds-barred bulletfest, as Mitchum shreds shoji screens and sword-wielding opponents with his hip-cradled shotgun.

And...

Street Fighter (Dir: Shigehiro Ozawa, 1974). Martial arts god Sonny Chiba at bone-crunching best.

King of New York (Dir: Abel Ferrara, 1990). Christopher Walken as NYC crime boss with headquarters in Waldorf-Astoria Hotel.

Emperor of the North Pole (Dir: Robert Aldrich, 1973). Brutal battle on hurtling freight train between King of the Hobos Lee Marvin and sadistic guard Ernest Borgnine.

Friends of Eddie Coyle (Dir: Peter Yates, 1973). Robert Mitchum trapped in Boston underworld.

Escape from New York (Dir: John Carpenter, 1981). Kurt Russell's Snake Plissken must save kidnapped President.

Walking Tall (Dir: Phil Karlson, 1973). Joe Don Baker is Sheriff Buford Pusser, a Southern lawman on the warpath.

The Asphalt Jungle (Dir: John Huston, 1950). Grity heist flick. One of the best.

Raging Bull (Dir: Martin Scorsese, 1980). See the Oscar-winning De Niro getting his face pummeled to burger meat.

Shaft (Dir: Gordon Parks, 1971). Hard-as-nails private eye John Shaft takes on Harlem underworld. With a name like Shaft . . . need we say more?

BADASS TUNES

If Music calms the Savage Beast, what effect could it possibly have on the badass?

The badass favors tunes that validate his worldview (for you students of philosophy, that's *Weltanschauung*). In other words, music that corresponds with his take-no-prisoners attitude. Badass music is defiant, angry, boastful, testosterone-laden. So skip the Donovan. Put away the Debbie Gibson. Sell or trade the Milli Vanilli. Here's a badass Desert Island List.

MUSIC FOR A BADASS ISLAND EXILE

Robert Johnson	*Hellhound on My Trail*
AC/DC	*Back in Black*
Queen	*Tie Your Mother Down*
Steppenwolf	*Born to Be Wild*
Iggy and The Stooges	*Search and Destroy*
Thin Lizzy	*The Boys are Back in Town*
Johnny Cash	*Folsom Prison Blues*
James Brown	*Cold Sweat*
Lynyrd Skynyrd	*That Smell*
Curtis Mayfied	*Superfly*
The Ramones	*Beat on the Brat*
Rolling Stones	*Dancin' with Mr D*
Screamin' Jay Hawkins	*I Put a Spell on You*
Alice Cooper	*Eighteen*
Peter Tosh	*Stepping Razor*
Link Wray	*Rumble*
Guns n' Roses	*Welcome to the Jungle*
Frank Sinatra	*One For My Baby (And One More for the Road)*
MC5	*Kick out the Jams*
John Lennon	*Cold Turkey*
Blind Lemon Jefferson	*See that My Grave is Kept Clean*
Ted Nugent	*Cat Scratch Fever*

NOTE: *You will never see a badass wearing earphones. By muffling the sounds of the quotidian, earphones interfere with the badass's well-developed "danger antennae." What's more, the average iPod or Walkman can easily be used against the wearer as an improvised weapon. Let your attention drift for a second, and that personal listening device can be ripped from your neck and raked across your jugular. So leave it at home. Work on your whistling and humming.*

BADASS DISCS

NWA	*Straight Outta Compton*
Led Zeppelin	*Led Zeppelin I*
Iggy Pop	*Lust For Life*
Stranglers	*No More Heroes*
Public Enemy	*It Takes a Nation of Millions to Hold us Back*
2Pac	*All Eyez on Me*
Black Sabbath	*Paranoid*
Nick Cave	*Murder Ballads*
Ice Cube	*AmeriKKKa's Most Wanted*
Albert King	*Born Under a Bad Sign*
Tom Waits	*Rain Dogs*
Sex Pistols	*Never Mind the Bollocks*
Frank Sinatra	*Only the Lonely*
Bruce Springsteen	*Born to Run*

BADASS READING MATERIAL

You can tell a lot about a man by what he has on his bedside table. No, we're not talking about hand lotion, the box of tissues, and the Barbie Benton issue of *Playboy*.

We're talking about pre-snooze ink. Some guys flip through the tax code while awaiting the Sandman; others peruse copies of the *Old Farmer's Almanac*. Some curl up with a *Mad* magazine compilation, others get droopy-eyed over a dog eared edition of the *Kelley Blue Book*.

Whatever the choice, the rule holds: Show us what a badass reads and we'll show you the badass.

Matt Bloom's *Blue Paradise*
Racing Form
Plutarch's *Parallel Lives*
William S. Burroughs' *Junky*
Des Pawson's *Handbook of Knots*
Norman Mailer's *Naked and the Dead*
Hustler
Mickey Spillane's *Kiss Me Deadly*
Sporting Knives 2004
Herman Melville's *Moby Dick*
Raymond Chandler's *The Big Sleep*
James Ellroy's *The Black Dahlia*
The Complete Guide to Navy SEAL Fitness
Bartlett's Quotations
Marine Corps Handbook
Book of Survival

BADASS LIVE ENTERTAINMENT

Yep, one trip to a concert venue or ball park will confirm your worst fears—it's a universe of clueless boneheads out there, all begging to be set straight by a dose of righteous badass fury. All things being equal, what's a badass to do?

- **Choose your entertainment options carefully.** You find yourself in a theme park, surrounded by screaming brats and their overweight parents, you have no one to blame but yourself.

- Venture out during off-hours.

- Avoid all-ages shows.

- Never spend so much on admission that you'll be reluctant to pack it up and move it when the swarming masses start to get your goat.

Try:
- The track
- Monster truck pulls
- Hot-dog/Pie-eating contests
- Miss Hawaiian Tropic beauty pageants
- Arm-wrestling tournaments
- Rock concerts (No one-name performers, e.g. Cher, Beyoncé)
- Wrestling, boxing, roller derby matches
- Strip clubs

- Maverick surfing
- Casinos and card clubs
- Skeet shooting
- Pit bull fighting
- Pool halls

WHERE A BADASS PUTS HIS HANDS DURING A LAP DANCE

An all-too-common dilemma. Most management frowns on customer-initiated contact with the girls. They would have you sit there, stock still, a bewildered grin on your face.

Management be damned: The badass must be true to himself. Help her in her gyrations. This is a performance—give her the audience feedback she needs. Anything else is, well, unnatural.

In short, *Put your hands wherever seems right.*

9

BADASS SEX

A SPOT QUIZ:

Q: What sets Man apart from the rest of the animal kingdom?

a. His self-consciousness
b. His empathy, i.e, his ability to care for and about others
c. His weakness for slapstick, pratfalls and Jerry Lewis
d. His raging libido
e. All of the above

The answer, of course, is (e). But if you're paying attention, you'll know that our subject here is sex. So let's focus on (d): Man's sex drive.

WARNING: What follows is not intended for children under twelve nor the weak of heart.

BADASS LIBIDO

As you probably know from personal experience, man is the only creature continuously in a state of estrus—otherwise known as "heat." Platypuses, hummingbirds, blue whales: These species have it easy. They get hot and bothered only once a year. Human beings, on the other hand, are horny 24/7, God bless us. So if you spend every waking moment (sleeping, as well) thinking about the Beast with two backs... well, you're not alone. To be horny is to be human (and vice versa).

We're not going to tell you how to have sex (we're assuming you paid attention in that special session of P.E. or watched *The Blue Lagoon* enough times to get the general idea). What we *are* going to do is give you some pointers that may help you survive the hormone hail-storm out there.

BADASS WOMEN

The pursuit of women is the engine that drives the train of civilization. It's the great, mad chase that makes the world go round. The frustrations, the ups and downs, the ins and outs, more ins and outs... it's endless.

Back in their day, badasses like Robert Mitchum and Lee Marvin always wound up in bed with hard-luck dames like Sherri North and Angie Dickinson. Blonde, brassy, tough-talkers. Voices a little hoarse from smoking. Whores with hearts of gold.

Times have changed. Thank God badass women haven't. The badass still likes his women BIG. Big hair. Big breasts. Big attitude. The bigger the better.

Luckily, fashion trends and advances in plastic surgery have made the 21st Century an eye-popping Paradise on Earth. A walk down any American street will turn up a jiggling assortment of C and D cups, all tethered beneath the tightest of cotton tops. For ass-men, the return of hip-huggers, miniskirts, short shorts, and thong underwear make life good. Very, very good.

It's a non-stop Mardi Gras parade out there—a badass just has to bring his beads.

WOMEN BADASSES LOVE

Pamela Anderson. A badass Goddess. Ignore the fact that she's Canadian.

Faith Hill. Pamela's goody-two shoes alter ego. Librarian crossed with sex kitten. If you're lucky, you'll get scratched

Lil' Kim. Remember to take your Vitamin E.

Salma Hayek. Ay, Chihuahua! We'd like to mutiny all over her bounty.

Denise Richards. Okay, so the Charlie Sheen connection is a bit of a turn-off. Can't we all just put that behind us?

Carmen Electra. She's no Madame Curie. But could Madame Curie cause grown men to weep? Using the talents God gave her.

Jennifer Love Hewitt. We thought only serial killers used their middle names.

Cameron Diaz. Like the girl next door—if the girl next door was an Amazon with an unbelievable ass.

Brooke Burke. Could someone please set up an All "Wild On" channel?

Heidi Klum. Not overexposed enough.

BADASS SEXUAL ETIQUETTE

As we've seen, even the simplest social encounters bring out the worst in the badass. All his training and instincts precondition the badass to expect to cause, and to be caused, pain. When we take this feral, watchful beast and plunge him into a benign social situation (especially one filled with the fairer sex), his adjustment period can be long, awkward, and arduous.

All our typical social cues have to be reconsidered. A hip check can be an invitation to dance, a grunt an offer of a drink, a head-butt a proposal of marriage. It's up to *you* to interpret correctly the signals he's sending.

SCENARIO #1

A crowded bar. Badass sidles up to an attractive brunette— she's wearing a Lycra sheath dress that fits her like the proverbial glove.

Without making eye contact, Badass jerks his head toward an empty ashtray in front of her and pulls a pack of Camel unfiltereds and a lighter out of his pocket. Did he just:

    a.   Offer to buy her a drink
    b.   Ask her to pass the ashtray
    c.   Offer her a cigarette
    d.   Ask her name
    e.   All of the above

ANSWER: e. (Hint: It's almost always "all of the above.")

The badass is a master of simplicity and sincerity. He says what he means and he means what he says. The bottom line is, he's trying to connect. Give the bastard some help.

BADASS PICK-UP LINES
(and How to Interpret Them)

"That your cigarette?"

What He Means: *I like the fact that you smoke. I'm too polite to point out the obvious connection between cigars and phalluses. We'll get around to that later.*

"You smell good."

What He Means: *I'd like to take a bath with you. Let's get clean before we get dirty.*

"Those puppies bite?"

What He Means: *Sex can be a battle of wills. You seem like a worthy opponent. Bring it on.* **And/Or** *You have beautiful breasts. When can I see them?*

"We'll talk... after I kick your ass in pool."

What He Means: *I'm comfortable letting you know that I like a competitive woman. And I'm only slightly neurotic about losing to one.*

"You barely legal?"

What He Means: *You look like the young Audrey Hepburn.* **And/Or** *I have unresolved issues concerning Girl Scout cookies.*

"What're you wearing under that dress? Jello?"

What He Means: *I've got a sweet tooth and I'm not ashamed to admit it.* **And/Or** *Hell of a body. When can I play with it?*

"You like hockey?"

What He Means: *We can bond over sports. But when push comes to shove, I'm going to work you over like a Zamboni.*

"You'd look damn good on the back of my Ducati."

What He Means: *I need you. And I'm not ashamed to admit it.*

"You drive standard... or automatic?"

What He Means: *I'll let you pretend to be in charge. And/Or How about warming me up with a handjob?*

"How'd you like to make the biggest mistake of your life tonight?"

What He Means: *A little humor goes a long way. The way to a woman's heart is through her smile... And/Or something like that.*

HEY BADASS!

The badass is the Great Unknown. He's as inscrutable as the Sphinx, as emotionally forthcoming as the Addams Family's Lurch. Compared to the legions of weepy hipsters and soul-searching yoga aficionados out there, the badass is in an emotive coma. His "giddy" is another man's flatline. The problem is, he likes it that way.

Dealing with the badass is an extreme sport. You've got to be in top condition, with the right equipment and a certain devil-may-care attitude. One approaches a badass the way one confronts a grizzly or a pit bull—with an open palm and heart, but with the full expectation of a serious mauling. Badasses will allow themselves to be petted, pampered, even to have their bellies scratched. But watch out: They can strike with terrifying speed and ferocity. Never forget: They're wild animals. You must be prepared to die.

Fact is, you're going to need a professional to guide you. Someone who is part fortune teller, part pop psychologist, part drill sergeant. Someone with nerves of steel and a heart of stone, who can lead you into the treacherous wilderness of Badass behavior and bring you out on the other side, grateful and unscathed.

Hey Badass: *It's my badass's birthday. How do I give him a gift in a way that's least likely to set him off?*

Catch him unawares, preferably when he's otherwise occupied or confined. For example, wait until he's working on his wheels. If he's down on his back, changing his oil, approach stealthily. Kick one of his boots, say "Hey," then drop the gift on the floor. Run.

Hey Badass: *My badass and I have been going out for a year. He's never said he loves me. What should I do?*

Stupid question. What do you mean, he's never said he loves you? Doesn't he grunt when you wish him good morning? Didn't he give you a sip of the last Mickey's Big Mouth the other day? What do you want? Chocolates?

Hey Badass: *How can I be sure I'm pleasing my badass in bed?*

One surefire clue is a ringing in your ears (caused by having your head banged into the headboard too many times).

Learn to interpret his grunts. There are grunts of boredom and grunts of pleasure. Remember, the onus is on you.

Final clue: badasses are as multiorgasmic as hamsters. When in doubt, assume he wants more.

Hey Badass: *I'm in charge of my company picnic and want my badass to help. How do I ask him?*

You must be kidding.

Hey Badass: *Whenever we go out to dinner, my badass insists on sitting at the back of the restaurant, facing the door. Why?*

He's keeping you alive, is what he's doing. The badass understands the world for what it is: a cesspool of fear and corruption. Bad guys are everywhere—all the badass can do is try to spot them before they spot him.

Surprise him sometime. Ask the maitre'd ahead of time for a secluded table, one with clear sight lines of the entrance and restrooms. When your server walks you over there, have him refer to it as "Your special bunker." That tic at the corner of your badass's mouth? That was a smile.

Hey Badass: *I'm so sick of my badass's clothes. How many white T-shirts can one man own? How do I get him to expand his wardrobe?*

What are we talking about here? Brooks Brothers button-down shirts? Seersucker pants? You trying to recreate Daddy? You want a Wall Street type, go to Wall Street. And God bless. You can't put a collar on a big cat and expect it to purr like a Siamese—you just get an angry big cat.

When you buy badass, you buy the whole package. Fashionista, heal thyself.

Hey Badass: *I want my badass to meet my parents. I realize this is a potentially explosive situation which must be handled delicately. Any advice?*

It seems like you're approaching D-Day with appropriate anxiety. That's a start. We're thinking public place. Lots of witnesses.

Convince your badass to go see a ball game or some wrestling matches. Have your parents buy the two adjacent seats. Put your mother next to your badass—he'll assume she's a kindly stranger. Have her compliment him on his tattoos. Have her offer to buy him a beer. Have her pay for his peanuts.

Say nothing. Then, as the crowd rises for the seventh-inning stretch, lean over and whisper to him,"Nice old lady." When he grunts his assent, add: "Yup. Good ol'

Mom." He'll wrinkle his brow, you'll smile, and the ice will be broken.

Good luck.

Hey Badass: *My badass seems to have lost interest in sex. What can I do?*

Are you sure he's really a badass?

Hey Badass: *I proposed to my badass and he accepted (I think). What kind of wedding should we plan?*

Badasses don't wear tuxes. You'll have to elope.

THE BADASS WAY
TO BREAK AN OPPONENT'S NOSE

No one, not even the most hard-core thug, likes having his nose broken. Chalk it up to vanity, queasiness at the sight of one's own blood, or the fact that it makes all your food taste like rust, but a broken schnoz is low on everyone's lists of favorites.

Which makes it the ideal badass counterattack.

The hardest part of your anatomy is your skull. You want to break an adversary's nose and make it stay broken, use your head (literally and figuratively).

1. Using the top of your head (never your forehead), drive into the middle of attacker's face. This can be done either facing toward or away from the adversary. Use legs and neck to increase power of head butt.

In most fights, the head butt works only once— your opponent (unless he's a drunken frat boy or an alien life form) tends to keep his distance after the initial blow. To finish the job, or just to add punctuation, we suggest wading in and delivering:

2. Elbow strike to proboscis.

3. As you walk away, avoid parting shots that'll teach you to keep your nose out of other people's business. These are cliché and bad form.

THE BADASS WAY

TO CLIMB THE OUTSIDE OF A BUILDING

We admit that chances are very, very slim that you'll ever have to climb up the outside of a building in an emergency. The chances of being hit by lighting or charged by a crazed rhino are much higher.

But that's our point: The badass must be prepared for anything and everything.

The key to this method is: Windows.

1. Open windows by smashing glass with shoe or fist. Cover fist with cloth and punch straight, snapping wrist back on contact.

2. Pull body up onto windowsill with arms. Elbows serve as "hooks," legs scurry for toeholds on building face.

3. Crawl onto ledge or windowsill and scan for next stage of ascent.

4. Make use of drainpipes. Hug with knees and shimmy up. Test-shake each section before applying full weight.

5. Take advantage of dangling telephone lines, television cables, banners.

6. No unnecessary swinging or heel-tapping.

7. On reaching objective, you're allowed to beat your chest like Tarzan. You've earned it.

THE BADASS WAY

TO SAVE YOURSELF FROM CHOKING

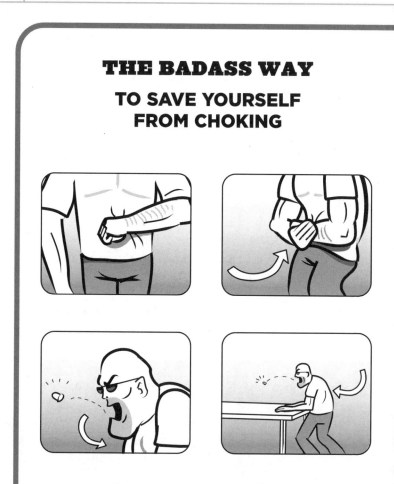

You're mid-joke at the company picnic when a section of all-beef frank lodges in your windpipe, cutting off your air supply. You gesture desperately at your throat, trying to communicate your plight. While your assembled co-workers kick into a half-hearted version of Charades ("Movie! Three words!"), your brain is starting to shut down.

Looks like you're going to have to save yourself.

We recommend the tried-and-true Heimlich maneuver.

1. Make a fist. Place thumb side against upper abdomen, between ribcage and navel.

2. Grab fist with opposite hand and jerk into upper abdomen with quick upward motion.

3. Repeat until offending frank is dislodged.

4. If alone at home, lean over table edge, couch or chair back and apply pressure. (Alternatively, hit self in abdomen with phone book, frying pan, Dachshund).

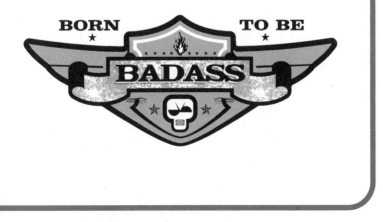

10

BADASS SPORTS

The badass is a natural, but discriminating, athlete. He can hold his own, if not excel, in most sports, but tends to avoid any involving racquets, paddles, or caddies. No curling, ping pong, or luge for the badass. He likes to hit and be hit.

BOXING

The sweet science: only it ain't sweet, and it sure ain't a science.

The fundamental rule of boxing has been and always will be to hit the other guy and avoid getting hit yourself—a principle near and dear to the badass's heart.

Take away the high profile title bouts, with all the attendant flash and glitz, and boxing remains the most primitive of the major spectator sports. Two men leaning forehead to forehead, attempting to pound one another into submission: The boxing ring is a spotlit crucible brimming over with blood, sweat, and muscle.

Hitting quotient: All there is

With weigh-in antics and chair-throwing participation of the fighters' respective entourages: Sweet indeed

HOCKEY

The verdict is out on this North-of-the-Border import. Hitting and fighting make it a natural badass selection; with the advent of TiVo, some even call the sport "All Fighting, All The Time."

There is plenty about the sport, however, to set one's remaining teeth on edge. The playoffs stretch on for months. The equipment (special pants, skates) is rounded, padded, feminine. The 'do-of-choice, the mullet, is as obsolete as Chia pets. The lights and fanfare are far too remi-

niscent of Ice Capades and Torville and Dean. Only sport with team named after a kid's flick.
Hitting quotient: High
With on-ice brawls: Very high

And then there's

FOOTBALL

If football did not exist,
it would be necessary to invent it.
—Voltaire

All right, so Voltaire didn't say that. But the point stands: Football is an inescapable fact of life. It's a fascinating metaphor for human conflict, intricate and bloody. It's a ritualized battle waged by surrogate armies on emerald fields every autumn week. It's a latter-day version of gladiatorial combat, with swarthy heroes battling one another to exhaustion and sometimes death. It's also a great excuse for a tail-gate party.

Football (and here we're talking the pros) is the badass sport *extraordinaire*. It takes all the things badasses value (honor, courage, grace under pressure) and packs them into a beer-guzzling, fist-pumping, cheerleader-ogling couple of hours. There's a lot to be said for the college game—nothing can rival the excitement caused by watching the men of your *alma mater* take the field (unless, of course, you went to Vassar). But college ball is, well, too damn clean (with the exception, of course, of the Southeastern Conference). For sheer blood and guts, nothing comes close to the NFL.

Some complain about the short length of the season. In our book, that just adds to the thrill of the game. Football must be played when the leaves are turning red, when rain and freezing slush turn the line of scrimmage into a muddy Maginot Line, when Thanksgiving is just around the corner and you can buy yourself a widescreen television as an early Christmas gift with impunity. Besides, what with added games on Mondays, Thursdays and, late in the season, even Saturdays, there's plenty of action packed into those few glorious months. The Super Bowl always comes too early for the true gridiron fan, and exhibition season seems light-years away.

And hitting? Football is smashmouth, brutal, primitive. John Madden (before he became a self-promoting caricature of himself) understood this—football, at its best, is a snarling, spitting, bloody mess. It's Beowulf versus Grendel, minus the mead and cod.

Hitting quotient: Through the roof

With on-field brawls: Tend to slow down the game and interfere with the legitimate violence

THE BADASS GUIDE TO BADASS GRIDIRON GODS

Dick Butkus. Eight Pro-Bowl appearances. Essence of middle linebacker. So badass, they named an award after him. They had to.

Jack Lambert. Two hundred seven pounds and 6 feet, 4 inches of "Nasty." Two-time NFL Defensive Player of the Year.

Joe Greene. Ten Pro Bowl appearances. His Meanness.

Ray Nitschke. Vicious Packer middle linebacker. Defined the position.

Ray Lewis. Has revived age-old alliance between the N.F.L. and J.A.I.L.

Mike Ditka. More or less perfected the tight end position.

Known for delivering blows to the trachea of anyone trying to defend him. Said it helped him make his cuts.

Jack Youngblood. Played title game and Super Bowl XIV against the Steelers with a fractured fibula. Played 201 consecutive games.

Bill Romanowski. Hits hard and keeps hitting... his teammates, that is.

Dick "Night Train" Lane. Cornerback made seven trips to the Pro Bowl. Terrifying open-field tackler.

THE BADASS GRIDIRON DUMBASS AWARD

Football is second only to boxing for spawning chest-pounding loudmouths pumped up on illegal substances and the smell of their opponent's blood—we're thinking of the antics of Mohawk-sporting, back-flipping Jorge "Maromero" Paez here.

Glancing back across the years, however, two pigskin blow-hards stand out. For sheer substance-abusing stupidity, it's a Mexican stand-off between Brian Bosworth and Mark Gastineau, two outstanding linebackers whose outsized personalities ultimately overshadowed their games. The Boz took the money and ran to the boney embrace of Hollywood, where he opines for UPN on the XFL, while Gastineau did a mid-season "sack-dance" into a cell at Rikers on a domestic violence rap.

In both cases, when the "steroid rage" stopped, so did the career.

SO, WHAT ABOUT...

BASEBALL

Once America's favorite pastime. Bloated, sluggish game played by bloated, sluggish players. Little premium placed on physical contact or effort, other than barreling over catcher when crossing home plate. The good guys make it look easy; the bad ones make it look excruciatingly boring.

Baseball players are second only to soccer players in their preening and hyperventilated injuries; a brush-back pitch is always grounds for an agitated (and usually spastic) rush toward the mound. Bench-emptying donnybrooks look more like a Labor Day sale at Filene's.

Hitting quotient: Low
With on-field brawls: Still low

BASKETBALL

Imagine an improvised kid's game such as dodge ball being yanked from the schoolyard and thrust onto the world stage. Suddenly this once innocent pastime is being played at the amateur, college, Olympic, and professional levels in front of millions of fans and is hauling in billions of dollars in revenue.

Sound far-fetched? But that's what's happened to basketball. The goofy P.E. game devised by James Naismith in 1891 to entertain his snowbound students is now second only to soccer as the world's most cherished sport. Crazy. Next thing you know, an actor or professional wrestler can become governor of a state.

Hoops has graduated from the schematic Cousy–Wooden team game to become a showcase for the prodigious individual athletic prowess of a handful of super humans (MJ, Shaq, Iverson). And while the badass can appreciate the finer points of the perimeter game, he prefers the rough-and-tumble Neo-Neanderthal offensive tactics of Detroit's "Bad Boys" and their twisted progeny, the early '90s Knicks. For sheer excitement, he'll take a good Charles Oakley moving-pick over a Kobe fade-away three-pointer anytime.

Hitting quotient: When played in the paint, extremely high

With courtside fisticuffs between irate fans throwing drinks and even more irate players whose feelings are easily hurt: Increases exponentially

NASCAR

A sport, or a corporate cash cow?

The one-time province of bootleggers and gear heads has become Wal-Mart-ized almost beyond recognition. Ever since the corporate suits got a whiff of racing's money-making potential, they've smothered it with advertising and product tie-ins. (Personally, we don't want Jeff Gordon or Dale Earnhardt, Jr. delivering our pizza; they should be out on the track where they belong.) Call us when NASCAR sheds the brands and gets back to fundamentals: speed, rubber and fuel.

Hitting quotient: Crashes and high-speed fender benders

ULTIMATE FIGHTING

Ultimate fighting has come a long way from the early '90s, when the glacial pace of the PPV matches could start to seem almost eerie, inhuman, like watching two anacondas trying to squeeze the life out of each other.

Nowadays, the emphasis in the UFC mixed martial arts spectacles is definitely on the "martial"--any sport that has a clause in its rulebook penalizing sticking your finger in any of your opponent's orifices is badass in our book.

Hitting quotient: Bring back eye gouging and fish-hooking.

AND THEN THERE'S...

WWE

The "E" stands for "entertainment." Vaudeville without the talent. Too much ring-time spent on Vince McMahon working out his personal demons.

X-TREME SPORTS

For pee-wee badasses. Dominated by guys whose voices haven't changed yet.

MOTOCROSS

Strictly for those who don't mind a little blood mixed with their urine.

TOUR DE FRANCE

How do you say, "My ass hurts" in French?

BADASS SPORTS ALTERNATIVES

Tired of all the incessant branding, logos, and high ticket prices that are choking the excitement out of organized sports? Want to get out there and break a sweat? Try these badass athletic actvities on for size.

WOOD-CHOPPING

Test your axe throwing talents. Perfect your springboard chop and hot saw talents while giving your upper body the workout of the century. Visit state fairs, reconstructed historical villages and maple festivals while you're at it.

SUICIDE HILL INDIAN HORSE RACE

Avoid getting trampled as you spur your horse 200 feet down Suicide Hill in Washington State, swim the Okanogan River, and clamber up the other bank. One minute of sheer slipping, sliding, frothy frenzy.

ARMWRESTLING FOR THE NEXT ROUND

No special equipment required. A badass classic.

SPEARHUNTING FERAL PIGS IN HAWAII

Pig in a poke, indeed. Shades of *Lord of the Flies*.

THE BADASS GUIDE TO EXERCISE

A QUIZ:

What are the only known natural enemies of the badass?

Cable TV pundits and porn stars shilling contraptions to enhance penis size, you say? True, but we were thinking more along the lines of gravity and aging. To paraphrase Samuel Butler: The way of all flesh is... southward. That's right: With each spin of the planet, the crow's feet around our eyes deepen and our flesh creeps down our torso towards our ankles. Call it The Badass Law of Thermodynamics: All muscle tone leads to a spare tire.

The badass battles back with exercise. We're not talking about working out in air-conditioned gyms (the weekend warriors are there to scope out chicks' leotard-clad asses, while the hardcore body-builders seem satisfied to check out each other). Nor are we talking about spending the nest egg on the raft of treadmills, isometric gew-gaws, and ergonomically-designed home systems resembling Klingon warships being hawked on late-night infomercials.

THE BADASS WORKOUT

The Badass Workout consists of only three exercises. That's right. Three. Like the Stooges. Or the blind mice.

Push-ups

Sit-ups

Pull-ups

The Push-Up

We do ours the Navy SEAL way:

Hands: A comfortable width apart—a little wider than the shoulders

Feet: Together

Back: Straight

Eyes: Looking forward

Lower yourself until there's less than a fist's width of room between your chest and the ground. Keep your back perfectly straight—don't let it sag or let your body bend at the waist. Repeat.

Feel the burn? Those are your biceps screaming out their thanks.

The Sit-Up

Start with your knees bent at a comfortable angle, hands clasped behind your head, elbows resting on the ground.

Come up, touch your elbows to your thighs, and return. Keep your back rounded. Repeat.

The Pull-Up

Grab the pull-up bar with your arms spaced a little wider than your shoulders. **NOTE:** Thumbs and fingers should be on the same side of the bar.

Look up. From a dead hang, pull yourself up and over the bar, keeping your back arched. **NOTE:** Think of your arms as hooks. Work your back, not your arms. And no leg motion or "bicycling"—legs must be still.

Lower yourself in a controlled manner and repeat.

There you have it—The Badass Workout. Basic but brutal. Combine reps of these exercises with a regular regimen of running (in boots, of course), and you have everything you need to keep yourself in ass-kicking shape until the day you drop.

So put the book down and get busy! You can read more when you're cooling down.

11

BADASS PETS

Every badass needs someone to confide in. But whom? Buddies look askance at intimacy— they'll think you want to borrow money. Girlfriends and wives are great, but sooner or later you're going to say too much and find yourself in a shitstorm without an umbrella. Shrinks cost too much, and priests, ministers, and rabbis have their own problems.

Every badass needs a pet. Tarzan had Cheetah, Timmy had Lassie, and Baretta had his cockatoo, Fred. Here are some of our favorite badass pets.

DOGS

"This one's a no-brainer," you're thinking. "The top badass dog has to be the pit bull. With a studded collar."

Yeah, well, you're WRONG. So pipe down and listen up.

The high testosterone pooches, breeds like pits, bulldogs, Great Danes, Presa Canarios, they're too damn obvious. They're primitive, drooling brutes with pea brains. Having one for a pet is like hanging out with a four-legged rugby player. The badass wants companionship, not competition.

The alternative, of course, is irony. (To the badass, "irony" is what you do when your shirt is wrinkled). The badass with the wry sense of humor may opt for the polar opposite of the droolers—dainty breeds like Chihuahuas, Lhasa apsos, miniature poodles.

"Ridiculous," you say.

I thought I told you to pipe down?

Of course it's ridiculous. That's the point. The delicacy of the dog serves only to emphasize the badass owner's badassedness, you see? It thwarts easy assumptions and overturns stereotypes. Besides, it's a guaranteed chick magnet, like pushing a baby carriage.

The problem with this approach is it requires too much forethought. (See **Cut-off button-down shirts**). And who really wants a Chihuahua for a pet?

In the final analysis, the ultimate badass pet is a scruffy mutt, a permanently chipper short-haired, cross-eyed, kink-tailed dingo mix saved from the pound. Eternally grateful. House-trained. Eager to fetch sticks, balls, newspapers. And in possession of enough simple tricks to impress the svelte brunette you brought home from the Christmas party.

> **VERDICT:** A great badass dog is a mixture of sidekick, straight man, body guard and confessor. Like Scooby Doo. Irreplaceable.

CATS

Big or little, cats are not badass pets. The badass may feed the occasional stray, but owning a cat is best left to Bond villains (Blofeld), boxers on the downward slope of their careers intent on pissing their fortunes away (Mike Tyson), or freaky Vegas lounge acts (Siegfried and Roy).

> **VERDICT:** Badasses do not change litter boxes. Particularly lion-sized ones. (If you must, get a Peterbald. Hairless, freaky. Looks like a crash-landed alien.)

And the rest:

FISH

Understated. Unexpected. And they can be flushed down the toilet or swallowed if you're forced to move suddenly.

> **VERDICT:** Badasses don't eat sushi and they don't befriend it, either. (If you must get a fish, get a tank of piranha. Great way to handle leftovers.)

BIRDS

Made popular by Robert Blake and Long John Silver. A bird in a cage is useless as a social prop—the badass wants one to perch on his shoulder and make smart-ass remarks to cops and women.

> **VERDICT:** Try getting a macaw to shut up when he's got a captive audience. (If you must, then get a penguin. Do you know *anyone* with a penguin?)

RODENTS

If you're looking for portability, avoid the cedar shavings gang (hamsters, gerbils, guinea pigs). Rats and mice are easily transportable and will eat whatever you're having.

> **VERDICT:** A controversial choice. The sad truth is, only guys admire rodents—chicks associate them with wretched poverty, bubonic plague, and horror movies. No one wants to hear their favorite Norway rat denounced as "filthy vermin." (If you must, then get a honey badger. Held to be the meanest critter extant.)

REPTILES

Basically miniature dinosaurs, with million-year-old chips on their shoulders. Reptiles are "cold-blooded" in every sense of the word. They spend their days under that plastic palm tree, plotting their means of escape and day-dreaming about a second Mesozoic era.

VERDICT: So-called vivarium pets have their fans. The badass is not among them. WARNING: Not to be trusted. Cover cage when viewing *Jurassic Park I–IV*. (If you must, then get a Komodo dragon. Doubles as watch-dog.)

INSECTS

See *Rodents*.

VERDICT: Sure-fire chick turn-off. (If you must, then get a death's head moth. But hide your sweaters and woolens.

BADASS PET NAMES

Brutus
Cain
Cerberus
Creature
Fang
Geronimo
Gilligan
In-Coming (Try shouting that.)
Killer

Mosca
Nero
Plague
Satan
Savage
Short Round
Sparky
Speck
Spike
Thing

12

BADASS BIBLE TRIAL BY FIRE FINAL EXAM™

Just how badass are you? We'll decide. Choose one answer for each of the following questions. Take your time. Use a #2 pencil only. Erase all mistakes—stray marks will be counted against you. And by all means be careful. The *Trial By Fire Final Exam* is like a driving test: Fuck it up and you have to wait a few months before you get to try again.

1. **Which of the following two-dimensional comic characters is a true badass?**
   a. Little Lulu
   b. The Incredible Hulk
   c. Richie Rich
   d. Sad Sack

2. **Which of the following three-dimensional comic characters is a true badass?**
   a. Conan O'Brien
   b. Arthur Conan Doyle
   c. Conan the Barbarian
   d. None of the above

3. **Your seaplane has crash-landed in the Alaskan bush, leaving you stranded hundreds of miles from the nearest habitation. The first thing you do is:**
   a. Rack your brains for recipes utilizing lichen and dirt
   b. Lay down and beat your fists on the ground
   c. Start humming Elton John and Kiki Dee's "Don't Go Breaking My Heart" maniacally
   d. Wrestle a grizzly for his freshly-caught salmon

4. **Your girlfriend is coming over for dinner. Rank the following steps in order of importance (most important first).**

a. Stash kitty litter box in closet
b. Dry toilet seat
c. Turn on ballgame
d. Take a nap

5. **Which of the following flicks would a badass not watch?**
   a. *Billy Jack*
   b. *Legend of the Drunken Master*
   c. *Fried Green Tomatoes*
   d. *The Good, the Bad and the Ugly*

6. **Which of the following is most likely to be uttered by a badass?**
   a. "Blistering Barnacles!"
   b. "Great Caesar's Ghost!"
   c. "Banzai!"
   d. "Gabba gabba hey!"

7. **Your sailboat is going down within sight of what seems to be a deserted island. Which of the following items do you take with you? Explain your reasoning.**
   a. Inflatable sex doll
   b. Swiss Army knife
   c. Frying pan
   d. Copy of Thomas Mann's *Magic Mountain*

8. **Spot the badass movie quotation.**
   a. "If they move, kill 'em."
   b. "I have come here to chew gum and kick ass... and I'm all out of bubble gum."
   c. "You talkin' to me?"
   d. All the above

9. Which event would a badass not attend?
   a. Tractor pull
   b. Gun show
   c. Séance
   d. Rugby match

10. Whose music could not be considered badass?
    a. Miles Davis
    b. Moby
    c. Metallica
    d. Moby Grape

11. Spot the badass foodstuff.
    a. Pop-Tarts
    b. Fried Spam
    c. Sushi
    d. Super Sugar Smacks

12. Which of the following is a badass vacation destination?
    a. Rock and Roll Hall of Fame
    b. Niagara Falls
    c. Legoland
    d. Six Flags Astroworld

13. Which of the following is not a Badass Rule of Thumb?
    a. "What chicks dig, adversaries will exploit"
    b. "Your belt should always match your shoes"
    c. "Keep it Simple"
    d. "Badasses don't wear cologne. On pain of death"

14. **Spot the Wild Card: Who isn't a badass?**
    a. Jackson Pollock
    b. Norman Mailer
    c. Norman Schwarzkopf
    d. Wally Cox

15. **Which of the following is not essential for survival?**
    a. Sex
    b. A complete set of skin care products by Aramis
    c. KA-Bar knife
    d. Zippo lighter

16. **Spot the badass breakfast.**
    a. Basil-tomato frittata with roasted potatoes and fresh-squeezed clementine juice
    b. Black coffee and a filterless cigarette
    c. Steel-cut Irish oatmeal and blueberries
    d. Met-Rx 100gm chocolate cookie dough bar and water

17. **Spot the badass.**
    a. Charles Baudelaire
    b. Charles Schulz
    c. Charles Bukowski
    d. Charles in Charge

18. **Which of the following is not a badass tattoo?**
    a. Skull and crossbones
    b. Betty Page on all fours
    c. Coiled rattlesnake
    d. Speed Racer, Chim Chim and Spritle

19. Which of the following is not an acceptable form of badass greeting?
    a. Kiss on both cheeks
    b. Soul handshake
    c. High five
    d. Head-butt

20. The badass's improvised weapon of choice is usually not a:
    a. Fish billy
    b. Broken chair leg
    c. Whiffle ball bat
    d. Pool cue

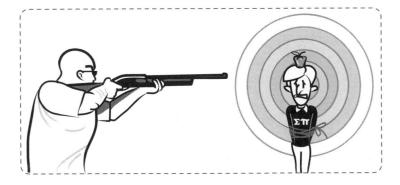

Answers:

1) b; 2) d; 3) d; 4) d,c,a,b; 5) c; 6) c; 7) a: It's a long swim to shore; 8) d; 9) c; 10) b; 11) b; 12) a; 13) b; 14) d; 15) b; 16) b; 17) c; 18) d; 19) a; 20) c.

Misses

0-1 Congratulations! Now go out and make us proud

2-5 You A.D.D. or something? Sit down and read it again. And concentrate this time.

5-10 Are you sure you're holding the book rightside up?

11-20 Sorry, but you're going to have to read *The Badass Bible* at least one more time.

www.badassbible.com

We've given you all the **BADASS BASICS**. If you're not up off the couch and out making the world safe for canned beer and one-handed push-ups, you've got no one to blame but yourself.

But there's something bothering you, isn't there? You feel restless, anxious, like a dog right before an earthquake. You want more **BADASS STUFF**...

So sit your badass down and log onto ww.badassbible.com for more of the down-and-dirty details essential to help you be the **BIGGEST BADASS** you can be.

It's babes, brawls and everything in between: an indispensible encyclopedia of **BADASS SKILLS** and information. From the squinty-eyed, snarling, ornery badasses who brought you *The Badass Bible*. **Now that's badass.**

CALLING ALL BADASSES

Got a favorite badass flick, bar, greasy spoon, or strip club to share with the Great Unwashed out there?

Send your inspiration to:
SKSmith@badassbible.com